The Reasonableness of Christianity, As Delivered in the Scriptures

By: John Locke

The Reasonableness of Christianity, As Delivered in the Scriptures

The little satisfaction and consistency that is to be found, in most of the systems of divinity I have met with, made me betake myself to the sole reading of the scriptures (to which they all appeal) for the understanding the Christian Religion. What from thence, by an attentive and unbiassed search, I have received, Reader, I here deliver to thee. If by this my labour thou receivest any light, or confirmation in the truth, join with me in thanks to the Father of lights, for his condescension to our understandings. If upon a fair and unprejudiced examination, thou findest I have mistaken the sense and tenour of the Gospel, I beseech thee, as a true Christian, in the spirit of the Gospel, (which is that of charity,) and in the words of sobriety, set me right, in the doctrine of salvation.

THE REASONABLENESS OF CHRISTIANITY, AS DELIVERED IN THE SCRIPTURES.

It is obvious to any one, who reads the New Testament, that the doctrine of redemption, and consequently of the gospel, is founded upon the supposition of Adam's fall. To understand, therefore, what we are restored to by Jesus Christ, we must consider what the scriptures show we lost by Adam. This I thought worthy of a diligent and unbiassed search: since I found the two extremes that men run into on this point, either on the one hand shook the foundations of all religion, or, on the other, made christianity almost nothing: for while some men would have all Adam's posterity doomed to eternal, infinite punishment, for the transgression of Adam, whom millions had never heard of, and no one had authorised to transact for him, or be his representative; this seemed to others so little consistent with the justice or goodness of the great and infinite God, that they thought there was no redemption necessary, and consequently, that there was none; rather than admit of it upon a supposition so derogatory to the honour and attributes of that infinite Being; and so made Jesus Christ nothing but the restorer and preacher of pure natural religion; thereby doing violence to the whole tenour of the New Testament. And, indeed, both sides will be suspected to have trespassed this way, against the written word of God, by any one, who does but take it to be a collection of writings, designed by God, for the instruction of the illiterate bulk of mankind, in the way to salvation; and therefore, generally, and in necessary points, to be understood in the plain direct meaning of the words and phrases: such as they may be supposed to have had in the mouths of the speakers, who used them according to the language of that time and country wherein they lived; without such learned, artificial, and forced senses of them, as are sought out, and put upon them, in most of the systems of divinity, according to the notions that each one has been bred up in.

To one that, thus unbiassed, reads the scriptures, what Adam fell from (is visible) was the state of perfect obedience, which is called justice in the New Testament; though the word, which in the original signifies justice, be translated righteousness: and by this fall he lost paradise, wherein was tranquillity and the tree of life; i. e. he lost bliss and immortality. The penalty annexed to the breach of the law, with the sentence pronounced by God upon it, show this. The penalty stands thus, Gen. ii. 17, "In the day that thou eatest thereof, thou shalt surely die." How was this executed? He did eat: but, in the day he did eat, he did not actually die; but was turned out of paradise from the tree of life, and shut out for ever from it, lest he should take thereof, and live for ever. This shows, that the state of paradise was a state of immortality, of life without end; which he lost that very day that he eat: his life began from thence to shorten, and waste, and to have an end; and from thence to his actual death, was but like the time of a prisoner, between the sentence passed, and the execution, which was in view and certain. Death then entered, and showed his face, which before was shut out, and not known. So St. Paul, Rom. v. 12, "By one man sin entered into the world, and death by sin;" i. e. a state of death and mortality: and, 1 Cor. xv. 22, "In Adam all die;" i. e. by reason of his transgression, all men are mortal, and come to die.

This is so clear in these cited places, and so much the current of the New Testament, that nobody can deny, but that the doctrine of the gospel is, that death came on all men by Adam's sin; only they differ about the signification of the word death: for some will have it to be a state of guilt, wherein not only he, but all his posterity was so involved, that every one descended of him deserved endless torment, in hell-fire. I shall say nothing more here, how far, in the apprehensions of men, this consists with the justice and goodness of God, having mentioned it above: but it seems a strange way of understanding a law, which requires the plainest and directest words, that by death should be meant eternal life in misery. Could any one be supposed, by a law, that says, "For felony thou shalt die;" not that he should lose his life; but be kept alive in perpetual, exquisite torments? And would any one think himself fairly dealt with, that was so used?

To this, they would have it be also a state of necessary sinning, and provoking God in every action that men do: a yet harder sense of the word death than the other. God says, that "in the day that thou eatest of the forbidden fruit, thou shalt die;" i. e. thou and thy posterity shall be, ever after, incapable of doing any thing, but what shall be sinful and provoking to me and shall justly deserve my wrath and indignation. Could a worthy man be supposed to put such terms upon the obedience of his subjects? Much less can the righteous God be supposed, as a punishment of one sin, wherewith he is displeased, to put man under the necessity of sinning continually, and so multiplying the provocation. The reason of this strange interpretation, we shall perhaps find, in some mistaken places of the New Testament. I must confess, by death here, I can understand nothing but a ceasing to be, the losing of all actions of life and sense. Such a death came on Adam, and all his posterity, by his first disobedience in paradise; under which death they should have lain for ever, had it not been for the redemption by Jesus Christ. If by death, threatened to Adam, were meant the corruption of human nature in his posterity, 'tis strange, that the New Testament should not any-where take notice of it, and tell us, that corruption seized on all, because of Adam's transgression, as well as it tells us so of death. But, as I remember, every one's sin is charged upon himself only.

Another part of the sentence was, "Cursed is the ground for thy sake: in sorrow shalt thou eat of it all the days of thy life; in the sweat of thy face shalt thou eat bread, till thou return unto the ground; for out of it wast thou taken; dust thou art, and to dust shalt thou return," Gen. iii. 17—19. This shows, that paradise was a place of bliss, as well as immortality; without drudgery, and without sorrow. But, when man was turned out, he was exposed to the toil, anxiety, and frailties of this mortal life, which should end in the dust, out of which he was made, and to which he should return: and then have no more life or sense, than the dust had, out of which he was made.

As Adam was turned out of paradise, so all his posterity were born out of it, out of the reach of the tree of life; all, like their father Adam, in a state of mortality, void of the tranquility and bliss of paradise. Rom. v. 12, "By one man sin entered into the world, and death by sin." But here will occur the common objection, that so many stumble at: "How doth it consist with the justice and goodness of God, that the posterity of Adam should suffer for his sin; the innocent be punished for the guilty?" Very well, if keeping one from what he has no right to, be called a punishment; the state of immortality, in paradise, is not due to the posterity of Adam, more than to any other creature. Nay, if God afford them a temporary, mortal life, 'tis his gift; they owe it to his bounty; they could not claim it as their right, nor does he injure them when he takes it from them. Had he taken from mankind any thing that was their right, or did he put men in a state of misery, worse than not being, without any fault or demerit of their own; this, indeed, would be hard to reconcile with the notion we have of justice; and much more with the goodness, and other attributes of the supreme Being, which he has declared of himself; and reason, as well as revelation, must acknowledge to be in him; unless we will confound good and evil, God and Satan. That such a state of extreme, irremediable torment is worse than no being at all; if every one's own sense did not determine against the vain philosophy, and foolish metaphysics of some men; yet our Saviour's peremptory decision, Matt. xxvi. 24, has put it past doubt, that one may be in such an estate, that it had been better for him not to have been born. But that such a temporary life, as we now have, with all its frailties and ordinary miseries, is better than no being, is evident, by the high value we put upon it ourselves. And therefore, though all die in Adam, yet none are truly punished, but for their own deeds. Rom. ii. 6, "God will render to every one," How? "According to his deeds. To those that obey unrighteousness, indignation and wrath, tribulation and anguish, upon every soul of man that doth evil," ver. 9. 2 Cor. v. 10, "We must appear before the judgment seat of Christ, that every one may receive the things done in his body, according to that he has done, whether it be good or bad." And Christ himself, who knew for what he should condemn men at the last day, assures us, in the two places, where he describes his proceeding at the great judgment, that the sentence of condemnation passes only upon the workers of iniquity, such as neglected to fulfil the law in acts of charity, Matt. vii. 23, Luke xiii. 27, Matt. xxv. 41, 42, &c. "And again, John v. 29, our Saviour tells the jews, that all shall come forth of their graves, they that have done good to the resurrection of life; and they that have done evil, unto the resurrection of damnation." But here is no condemnation of any one, for what his fore-father Adam had done; which it is not likely should have been omitted, if that should have been a cause why any one was adjudged to the fire, with the devil and his angels. And he tells his disciples, that when he comes again with his angels, in the glory of his Father, that then he will render to every one according to his works, Matt. xvi. 27.

Adam being thus turned out of paradise, and all his posterity born out of it, the consequence of it was, that all men should die, and remain under death for ever, and so be utterly lost.

From this estate of death, Jesus Christ restores all mankind to life; 1 Cor. xv. 22, "As in Adam all die, so in Christ shall all be made alive." How this shall be, the same apostle tells us in the foregoing ver. 21. "By man death came, by man also came the resurrection from the dead." Whereby it appears, that the life, which Jesus Christ restores to all men, is that life, which they receive again at the resurrection. Then they recover from death, which otherwise all mankind should have continued under, lost for ever; as appears by St. Paul's arguing, 1 Cor. xv. concerning the resurrection.

And thus men are, by the second Adam, restored to life again; that so by Adam's sin they may none of them lose any thing, which by their own righteousness they might have a title to: for righteousness, or an exact obedience to the law, seems, by the scripture, to have a claim of right to eternal life, Rom. iv. 4. "To him that worketh," i. e. does the works of the law, "is the reward not reckoned of grace, but of debt." And Rev. xxii. 14, "Blessed are they who do his commandments, that they may have right to the tree of life, which is in the paradise of God." If any of the posterity of Adam were just, they shall not lose the reward of it, eternal life and bliss, by being his mortal issue: Christ will bring them all to life again; and then they shall be put every one upon his own trial, and receive judgment, as he is found to be righteous, or not. And the righteous, as our Saviour says, Matt. xxv. 46, shall go into eternal life. Nor shall any one miss it, who has done, what our Saviour directed the lawyer, who asked, Luke x. 25, What he should do to inherit eternal life? "Do this," i. e. what is required by the law, "and thou shalt live."

On the other side, it seems the unalterable purpose of the divine justice, that no unrighteous person, no one that is guilty of any breach of the law, should be in paradise: but that the wages of sin should be to every man, as it was to Adam, an exclusion of him out of that happy state of immortality, and bring death upon him. And this is so conformable to the eternal and established law of right and wrong, that it is spoken of too, as if it could not be otherwise. St. James says, chap. i. 15, "Sin, when it is finished, bringeth forth death," as it were, by a natural and necessary production. "Sin entered into the world, and death by sin," says St. Paul, Rom. v. 12: and vi. 23, "The wages of sin is death." Death is the purchase of any, of every sin. Gal. iii. 10, "Cursed is every one, who continueth not in all things which are written in the book of the law to do them." And of this St. James gives a reason, chap. ii. 10, 11, "Whosoever shall keep the whole law, and yet offend in one point, he is guilty of all: for he that said, Do not commit adultery, said also, Do not kill:" i. e. he that offends in any one point, sins against the authority which established the law.

Here then we have the standing and fixed measures of life and death. Immortality and bliss, belong to the righteous; those who have lived in an exact conformity to the law of God, are out of the reach of death; but an exclusion from paradise and loss of immortality is the portion of sinners; of all those who have any way broke that law, and failed of a complete obedience to it, by the guilt of any one transgression. And thus mankind by the law are put upon the issues of life or death, as they are righteous or unrighteous, just, or unjust; i. e. exact performers or transgressors of the law.

But yet, "all having sinned," Rom. iii. 23, "and come short of the glory of God," i. e. the kingdom of God in heaven, (which is often called his glory,) "both jews and gentiles;" ver. 22, so that, "by the deeds of the law," no one could be justified, ver. 20, it follows, that no one could then have eternal life and bliss.

Perhaps, it will be demanded, "Why did God give so hard a law to mankind, that to the apostle's time no one of Adam's issue had kept it? As appears by Rom. iii. and Gal. iii. 21, 22."

Answ. It was such a law as the purity of God's nature required, and must be the law of such a creature as man; unless God would have made him a rational creature, and not required him to have lived by the law of reason; but would have countenanced in him irregularity and disobedience to that light which he had, and that rule which was suitable to his nature; which would have been to have authorised disorder, confusion, and wickedness in his creatures: for that this law was the law of reason, or as it is called, of nature; we shall see by and by: and if rational creatures will not live up to the rule of their reason, who shall excuse them? If you will admit them to forsake reason in one point, why not in another? Where will you stop? To disobey God in any part of his commands, (and 'tis he that commands what reason does,) is direct rebellion; which, if dispensed with in any point, government and order are at an end; and there can be no bounds set to the lawless exorbitancy of unconfined man. The law therefore was, as St. Paul tells us, Rom. vii. 12, "holy, just, and good," and such as it ought, and could not otherwise be.

This then being the case, that whoever is guilty of any sin should certainly die, and cease to be; the benefit of life, restored by Christ at the resurrection, would have been no great advantage, (for as much as, here again, death must have seized upon all mankind, because all have sinned; for the wages of sin is everywhere death, as well after as before the resurrection,) if God had not found out a way to justify some, i. e. so many as obeyed another law, which God gave; which in the New Testament is called "the law of faith," Rom. iii. 27, and is opposed to "the law of works." And therefore the punishment of those who would not follow him, was to lose their souls, i. e. their lives, Mark viii. 35—38, as is plain, considering the occasion it was spoke on.

The better to understand the law of faith, it will be convenient, in the first place, to consider the law of works. The law of works then, in short, is that law which requires perfect obedience, without any remission or abatement; so that, by that law, a man cannot be just, or justified, without an exact performance of every tittle. Such a perfect obedience, in the New Testament, is termed δικαιοσύνη, which we translate righteousness.

The language of this law is, "Do this and live, transgress and die." Lev. xviii. 5, "Ye shall keep my statutes and my judgments, which if a man do, he shall live in them." Ezek. xx. 11, "I gave them my statutes, and showed them my judgments, which if a man do, he shall even live in them. Moses, says St. Paul, Rom. x. 5, describeth the righteousness, which is of the law, that the man, which doth these things, shall live in them." Gal. iii. 12, "The law is not of faith; but that man, that doth them, shall live in them." On the other side, transgress and die; no dispensation, no atonement. Ver-10, "Cursed is every one that continueth not in all things which are written in the book of the law to do them."

Where this law of works was to be found, the New Testament tells us, viz. in the law delivered by Moses, John i. 17, "The law was given by Moses, but grace and truth came by Jesus Christ." Chap. vii. 19, "Did not Moses give you the law?" says our Saviour, "and yet none of you keep the law." And this is the law, which he speaks of, where he asks the lawyer, Luke x. 26. "What is written in the law? How readest thou? ver. 28, This do, and thou shalt live." This is that which St. Paul so often styles the law, without any other distinction, Rom. ii. 13, "Not the hearers of the law are just before God, but the doers of the law are justified." 'Tis needless to quote any more places; his epistles are full of it, especially this of the Romans.

"But the law given by Moses, being not given to all mankind, how are all men sinners; since, without a law, there is no transgression?" To this the apostle, ver. 14, answers, "For when the gentiles, which have not the law, do (i. e. find it reasonable to do) by nature the things contained in the law; these, having not the law, are a law unto themselves; which show the work of the law written in their hearts; their consciences also bearing witness, and amongst themselves their thoughts accusing or excusing one another." By which, and other places in the following chapter, 'tis plain, that under the law of works, is comprehended also the law of nature, knowable by reason, as well as the law given by Moses. For, says St. Paul, Rom. iii. 9, 23, "We have proved both jews and gentiles, that they are all under sin: for all have sinned, and come short of the glory of God:" which they could not do without a law.

Nay, whatever God requires any-where to be done, without making any allowance for faith, that is a part of the law of works: so that forbidding Adam to eat of the tree of knowledge was part of the law of works. Only we must take notice here, that some of God's positive commands, being for peculiar ends, and suited to particular circumstances of times, places, and persons; have a limited and only temporary obligation by virtue of God's positive injunction; such as was that part of Moses's law, which concerned the outward worship or political constitution of the jews; and is called the ceremonial and judicial law, in contradistinction to the moral part of it: which being conformable to the eternal law of right, is of eternal obligation; and therefore remains in force still, under the gospel; nor is abrogated by the law of faith, as St. Paul found some ready to infer, Rom. iii. 31, "Do we then make void the law, through faith? God forbid: yea we establish the law."

Nor can it be otherwise: for, were there no law of works, there could be no law of faith. For there could be no need of faith, which should be counted to men for righteousness; if there were no law, to be the rule and measure of righteousness, which men failed in their obedience to. Where there is no law, there is no sin; all are righteous equally, with or without faith.

The rule, therefore, of right, is the same that ever it was; the obligation to observe it is also the same: the difference between the law of works, and the law of faith, is only this: that the law of works makes no allowance for failing on any occasion. Those that obey are righteous; those that in any part disobey, are unrighteous, and must not expect life, the reward of righteousness. But, by the law of faith, faith is allowed to supply the defect of full obedience: and so the believers are admitted to life and immortality, as if they were righteous. Only here we must take notice, that when St. Paul says, that the gospel establishes the law, he means the moral part of the law of Moses; for that he could not mean the ceremonial, or political part of it, is evident, by what I quoted out of him just now, where he says, That the gentiles do, by nature, the things contained in the law, their consciences bearing witness. For the gentiles neither did, nor thought of, the judicial or ceremonial institutions of Moses; 'twas only the moral part their consciences were concerned in. As for the rest, St. Paul tells the Galatians, chap. iv. they are not under that part of the law, which ver. 3, he calls elements of the world; and ver. 9, weak and beggarly elements. And our Saviour himself, in this gospel sermon on the mount, tells them, Matt. v. 17, That, whatever they might think, he was not come to dissolve the law, but to make it more full and strict: for that which is meant by πληρῶσαι is evident from the following part of that chapter, where he gives the precepts in a stricter sense, than they were received in before. But they are all precepts of the moral law, which he re-inforces. What should become of the ritual law, he tells the woman of Samaria, in these words, John iv. 21, 23, "The hour cometh, when you shall, neither in this mountain, nor yet at Jerusalem, worship the Father. But the true worshippers shall worship the Father in spirit and in truth; for the Father seeketh such to worship him."

Thus then, as to the law, in short: the civil and ritual part of the law, delivered by Moses, obliges not christians, though, to the jews, it were a part of the law of works; it being a part of the law of nature, that man ought to obey every positive law of God, whenever he shall please to make any such addition to the law of his nature. But the moral part of Moses's law, or the moral law, (which is every-where the same, the eternal rule of right,) obliges christians, and all men, every-where, and is to all men the standing law of works. But christian believers have the privilege to be under the law of faith too; which is that law, whereby God justifies a man for believing, though by his works he be not just or righteous, i. e. though he come short of perfect obedience to the law of works. God alone does or can justify, or make just, those who by their works are not so: which he doth, by counting their faith for righteousness, i. e. for a complete performance of the law. Rom. iv. 3, "Abraham believed God, and it was counted to him for righteousness." Ver. 5, "To him that believeth on him that justifieth the ungodly, his faith is counted for righteousness." Ver. 6, "Even as David also describeth the blessedness of the man unto whom God imputeth righteousness without works;" i. e. without a full measure of works, which is exact obedience. Ver. 7, Saying, "Blessed are they whose iniquities are forgiven, and whose sins are covered." Ver. 8, "Blessed is the man, to whom the Lord will not impute sin."

This faith, for which God justified Abraham, what was it? It was the believing God, when he engaged his promise in the covenant he made with him. This will be plain to any one, who considers these places together, Gen. xv. 6, "He believed in the Lord, or believed the Lord." For that the Hebrew phrase, "believing in," signifies no more but believing, is plain from St. Paul's citation of this place, Rom. iv. 3, where he repeats it thus: "Abraham believed God," which he thus explains, ver. 18—22, "Who against hope believed in hope, that he might become the father of many nations: according to that which was spoken, So shall thy seed be. And, being not weak in faith, he considered not his own body now dead, when he was about an hundred years old, nor yet the deadness of Sarah's womb. He staggered not at the promise of God, through unbelief; but was strong in faith giving glory to God. And being fully persuaded, that what he had promised he was also able to perform. And therefore it was imputed to him for righteousness." By which it is clear, that the faith which God counted to Abraham for righteousness, was nothing but a firm belief of what God declared to him; and a steadfast relying on him, for the accomplishment of what he had promised.

"Now this," says St. Paul, ver. 23, 24, "was not writ for his [Abraham's] sake alone, but for us also;" teaching us, that as Abraham was justified for his faith, so also ours shall be accounted to us for righteousness, if we believe God, as Abraham believed him. Whereby it is plain is meant the firmness of our faith, without staggering, and not the believing the same propositions that

Abraham believed; viz. that though he and Sarah were old, and past the time and hopes of children, yet he should have a son by her, and by him become the father of a great people, which should possess the land of Canaan. This was what Abraham believed, and was counted to him for righteousness. But nobody, I think, will say, that any one's believing this now, shall be imputed to him for righteousness. The law of faith then, in short, is for every one to believe what God requires him to believe, as a condition of the covenant he makes with him: and not to doubt of the performance of his promises. This the apostle intimates in the close here, ver. 24, "But for us also, to whom it shall be imputed, if we believe on him that raised up Jesus our Lord from the dead." We must, therefore, examine and see what God requires us to believe now, under the revelation of the gospel; for the belief of one invisible, eternal, omnipotent God, maker of heaven and earth, &c. was required before, as well as now.

What we are now required to believe to obtain eternal life, is plainly set down in the gospel. St. John tells us, John iii. 36, "He that believeth on the Son, hath eternal life; and he that believeth not the Son, shall not see life." What this believing on him is, we are also told in the next chapter: "The woman said unto him, I know that the Messiah cometh: when he is come, he will tell us all things. Jesus saith unto her, I that speak unto thee, am he. The woman then went into the city, and saith to the men, come see a man that hath told me all things that ever I did: is not this the Messiah? and many of the Samaritans believed on him for the saying of the woman, who testified, he told me all that ever I did. So when the Samaritans were come unto him, many more believed because of his words, and said to the woman, We believe not any longer, because of thy saying; for we have heard ourselves, and we know that this man is truly the Saviour of the world, the Messiah." John iv. 25, 26, 29, 39, 40, 41, 42.

By which place it is plain, that believing on the Son is the believing that Jesus was the Messiah; giving credit to the miracles he did, and the profession he made of himself. For those who are said to believe on him, for the saying of the woman, ver. 39, tell the woman that they now believed not any longer, because of her saying: but that having heard him themselves, they knew, i. e. believed, past doubt, that he was the Messiah.

This was the great proposition that was then controverted, concerning Jesus of Nazareth, "Whether he was the Messiah or no?" And the assent to that was that which distinguished believers from unbelievers. When many of his disciples had forsaken him, upon his declaring that he was the bread of life, which came down from heaven, "He said to his apostles, Will ye also go away?" Then Simon Peter answered him, "Lord, to whom shall we go? Thou hast the words of eternal life. And we believe, and are sure, that thou art the Messiah, the Son of the living God," John vi. 69. This was the faith which distinguished them from apostates and unbelievers, and was sufficient to continue them in the rank of apostles: and it was upon the same proposition, "That Jesus was the Messiah, the Son of the living God," owned by St. Peter, that our Saviour said, he would build his church, Matt. xvi. 16—18.

To convince men of this, he did his miracles; and their assent to, or not assenting to this, made them to be, or not to be, of his church; believers, or not believers: "The jews came round about him, and said unto him, How long dost thou make us doubt? If thou be the Messiah, tell us plainly. Jesus answered them, I told you, and ye believed not: the works that I do in my Father's name, they bear witness of me. But ye believe not, because ye are not of my sheep," John x.

24—26. Conformable hereunto, St. John tells us, that "many deceivers are entered into the world, who confess not that Jesus, the Messiah, is come in the flesh. This is a deceiver and an antichrist; whosoever abideth not in the doctrine of the Messiah, has not God. He that abideth in the doctrine of the Messiah," i. e. that Jesus is he, "hath both the Father and the Son," 2 John 7, 9. That this is the meaning of the place, is plain from what he says in his foregoing epistle, "Whosoever believeth that Jesus is the Messiah, is born of God," 1 John v. 1. And therefore, drawing to a close of his gospel, and showing the end for which he writ it, he has these words: "Many other signs truly did Jesus in the presence of his disciples, which are not written in this book: but these are written that ye may believe that Jesus is the Messiah, the Son of God; and that believing, you might have life through his name," John xx. 30, 31. Whereby it is plain, that the gospel was writ to induce men into a belief of this proposition, "That Jesus of Nazareth was the Messiah;" which if they believed, they should have life.

Accordingly the great question among the jews was, whether he were the Messiah or no? and the great point insisted on and promulgated in the gospel, was, that he was the Messiah. The first glad tidings of his birth, brought to the shepherds by an angel, was in these words: "Fear not: for, behold, I bring you good tidings of great joy, which shall be to all people: for to you is born this day, in the city of David, a Saviour, who is the Messiah, the Lord," Luke ii. 11. Our Saviour discoursing with Martha about the means of attaining eternal life, saith to her, John xi. 27, "Whosoever believeth in me, shall never die. Believest thou this? She saith unto him, Yea, Lord, I believe that thou art the Messiah, the Son of God, which should come into the world." This answer of hers showeth, what it is to believe in Jesus Christ, so as to have eternal life; viz. to believe that he is the Messiah, the son of God, whose coming was foretold by the prophets. And thus Andrew and Philip express it: Andrew says to his brother Simon, "we have found the Messiah, which is, being interpreted, the Christ. Philip saith to Nathanael, we have found him, of whom Moses in the law and the prophets did write, Jesus of Nazareth, the son of Joseph," John i. 41, 45. According to what the evangelist says in this place, I have, for the clearer understanding of the scripture, all along put Messiah for Christ: Christ being but the Greek name for the Hebrew Messiah, and both signifying the Anointed.

And that he was the Messiah, was the great truth he took pains to convince his disciples and apostles of; appearing to them after his resurrection: as may be seen, Luke xxiv. which we shall more particularly consider in another place. There we read what gospel our Saviour preached to his disciples and apostles: and that as soon as he was risen from the dead, twice, the very day of his resurrection.

And, if we may gather what was to be believed by all nations from what was preached unto them, we may certainly know what they were commanded, Matt. ult. to teach all nations, by what they actually did teach all nations. We may observe, that the preaching of the apostles every-where in the Acts, tended to this one point, to prove that Jesus was the Messiah. Indeed, now, after his death, his resurrection was also commonly required to be believed, as a necessary article, and sometimes solely insisted on: it being a mark and undoubted evidence of his being the Messiah, and necessary now to be believed by those who would receive him as the Messiah. For since the Messiah was to be a Saviour and a king, and to give life and a kingdom to those who received him, as we shall see by and by; there could have been no pretence to have given him out for the Messiah, and to require men to believe him to be so, who thought him under the power of death, and corruption of the grave. And therefore those who believed him to be the Messiah, must believe that he was risen from the dead: and those who believed him to be risen from the dead, could not doubt of his being the Messiah. But of this more in another place.

Let us see therefore, how the apostles preached Christ, and what they proposed to their hearers to believe. St. Peter at Jerusalem, Acts ii. by his first sermon, converted three thousand souls. What was his word, which, as we are told, ver. 41, "they gladly received, and thereupon were baptized?" That may be seen from ver. 22 to 36. In short, this; which is the conclusion, drawn from all that he had said, and which he presses on them, as the thing they were to believe, viz. "Therefore let all the house of Israel know assuredly, that God hath made that same Jesus, whom ye have crucified, Lord and Messiah," ver. 36.

To the same purpose was his discourse to the jews, in the temple, Acts iii. the design whereof you have, ver. 18. "But those things that God before had showed, by the mouth of all his prophets, that the Messiah should suffer, he hath so fulfilled."

In the next chapter, Acts iv. Peter and John being examined, about the miracle on the lame man, profess it to have been done in the name of Jesus of Nazareth, who was the Messiah, in whom alone there was salvation, ver. 10—12. The same thing they confirm to them again, Acts v. 29— 32. "And daily in the temple, and in every house, they ceased not to teach and preach Jesus the Messiah," ver. 42.

What was Stephen's speech to the council, Acts vii. but a reprehension to them that they were the betrayers and murderers of the Just One? Which is the title, by which he plainly designs the Messiah whose coming was foreshown by the prophets, ver. 51, 52. And that the Messiah was to be without sin, (which is the import of the word Just,) was the opinion of the jews, appears from John ix. ver. 22, compared with 24.

Act viii. Philip carries the gospel to Samaria: "Then Philip went down to Samaria, and preached to them." What was it he preached? You have an account of it in this one word, "the Messiah," ver. 5. This being that alone which was required of them, to believe that Jesus was the Messiah; which when they believed they were baptized. "And when they believed Philip's preaching the gospel of the kingdom of God, and the name of Jesus the Messiah, they were baptized, both men and women." ver. 12.

Philip being sent from thence by a special call of the Spirit, to make an eminent convert; out of Isaiah preaches to him Jesus, ver. 35. And what it was he preached concerning Jesus, we may know by the profession of faith the eunuch made, upon which he was admitted to baptism, ver. 37. "I believe that Jesus Christ is the Son of God:" which is as much as to say, I believe that he, whom you call Jesus Christ, is really and truly the Messiah, that was promised. For, that believing him to be the Son of God, and to be the Messiah, was the same thing, may appear, by comparing John i. 45, with ver. 49, where Nathanael owns Jesus to be the Messiah, in these terms: "Thou art the Son of God; thou art the king of Israel." So the jews, Luke xxii. 70, asking Christ, whether he were the Son of God, plainly demanded of him, whether he were the Messiah? Which is evident, by comparing that with the three preceding verses. They ask him, ver. 67, Whether he were the Messiah? He answers, "If I tell you, you will not believe:" but withal tells them, that from thenceforth he should be in possession of the kingdom of the Messiah, expressed in these words, ver. 69. "Hereafter shall the Son of Man sit on the right hand of the power of God:" which made them all cry out, "Art thou then the Son of God?" i. e. Dost thou then own thyself to be the Messiah? To which he replies, "Ye say that I am." That the Son of God was the known title of the Messiah at that time, amongst the jews, we may see also from what the jews say to Pilate, John xix. 7. "We have a law, and by our law he ought to die, because he made himself the Son of God;" i. e. by making himself the Messiah, the prophet which was to come, but falsely; and therefore he deserves to die by the law, Deut. xviii. 20. That this was the common signification of the Son of God, is farther evident, from what the chief priests, mocking him, said, when he was on the cross, Matt. xxvii. 42. "He saved others, himself he cannot save: if he be the king of Israel, let him now come down from the cross, and we will believe him. He trusted in God, let him deliver him now, if he will have him; for he said, I am the Son of God;" i. e. He said, he was the Messiah: but 'tis plainly false; for, if he were, God would deliver him: for the Messiah is to be king of Israel, the Saviour of others; but this man cannot save himself. The chief priests mention here the two titles, then in use, whereby the jews commonly designed the Messiah, viz. "Son of God, and king of Israel." That of Son of God was so familiar a compellation of the Messiah, who was then so much expected and talked of, that the Romans, it seems, who lived amongst them, had learned it, as appears from ver. 54. "Now when the centurion and they that were with him, watching Jesus, saw the earthquake, and those things that were done, they feared greatly, saying, truly this was the Son of God;" this was that extraordinary person that was looked for.

Acts ix. St. Paul, exercising the commission to preach the gospel, which he had received in a miraculous way, ver. 20. "Straitway preached Christ in the synagogues, that he is the Son of God;" i. e. that Jesus was the Messiah: for Christ, in this place, is evidently a proper name. And that this was it, which Paul preached, appears from ver. 22. "Saul increased the more in strength, and confounded the jews, who dwelt in Damascus, proving that this is the very Christ," i. e. the Messiah.

Peter, when he came to Cornelius at Cæsarea, who, by a vision, was ordered to send for him, as St. Peter on the other side was by a vision commanded to go to him; what does he teach him? His whole discourse, Acts x. tends to show what, he says, God commanded the apostles, "To preach unto the people, and to testify, that it is he [Jesus] which was ordained of God to be the judge of the quick and the dead. And that it was to him, that all the prophets give witness, that, through his name, whosoever believeth in him, shall have remission of sins," ver. 42, 43. "This is the word, which God sent to the children of Israel; that word, which was published throughout all Judea, and began from Galilee, after the baptism which John preached," ver. 36, 37. And these are the words, which had been promised to Cornelius, Acts xi. 14, "Whereby he and all his house should be saved:" which words amount only to thus much: that Jesus was the Messiah, the Saviour that was promised. Upon their receiving of this, (for this was all was taught them,) the Holy Ghost fell on them, and they were baptized. 'Tis observable here, that the Holy Ghost fell on them, before they were baptized, which, in other places, converts received not till after baptism. The reason whereof seems to be this, that God, by bestowing on them the Holy Ghost, did thus declare from Heaven, that the gentiles, upon believing Jesus to be the Messiah, ought to be admitted into the church by baptism, as well as the jews. Whoever reads St. Peter's defence, Acts xi. when he was accused by those of the circumcision, that he had not kept that distance, which he ought, with the uncircumcised, will be of this opinion; and see by what he says, ver. 15, 16, 17, that this was the ground, and an irresistible authority to him for doing so strange a thing, as it appeared to the jews, (who alone yet were members of the christian church,) to admit gentiles into their communion, upon their believing. And therefore St. Peter, in the foregoing chapter, Acts x. before he would baptize them, proposes this question, "to those of the circumcision, which came with him, and were astonished, because that on the gentiles also was poured out the gift of the Holy Ghost: can any one forbid water, that these should not be baptized, who have received the Holy Ghost as well as we?" ver. 47. And when some of the sect of the pharisees, who believed, thought it needful that the converted gentiles should be circumcised and keep the law of Moses, Acts xv. "Peter rose up and said unto them, men and brethren, you know that a good while ago God made choice amongst us, that the gentiles," viz. Cornelius, and those here converted with him, "by my mouth should hear the gospel and believe. And God, who knoweth the hearts, bare them witness, giving them the Holy Ghost, even as he did unto us, and put no difference between us and them, purifying their hearts by faith," v. 7—9. So that both jews and gentiles, who believed Jesus to be the Messiah, received thereupon the seal of baptism; whereby they were owned to be his, and distinguished from unbelievers. From what is above said, we may observe that this preaching Jesus to be the Messiah is called the Word, and the Word of God: and believing it, receiving the Word of God. Vid. Acts x. 36, 37. and xi. 1, 19, 20. and the word of the gospel, Acts xv. 7. And so likewise in the history of the gospel, what Mark, chap. iv. 14, 15, calls simply the word, St. Luke calls the word of God, Luke viii. 11. And St. Matthew, chap. xiii. 19, the word of the kingdom; which were, it seems, in the gospel-writers synonymous terms, and are so to be understood by us.

But to go on: Acts xiii. Paul preaches in the synagogue at Antioch, where he makes it his business to convince the jews, that "God, according to his promise, had of the seed of David raised to Israel a Saviour Jesus." v. 24. That he was He of whom the prophets writ, v. 25—29, i. e. the Messiah: and that, as a demonstration of his being so, God had raised him from the dead, v. 30. From whence he argues thus, v. 32, 33. We evangelize to you, or bring you this gospel, "how that the promise which was made to our fathers, God hath fulfilled the same unto us, in that he hath raised Jesus again;" as it is also written in the second psalm, "Thou art my Son, this day I have begotten thee." And having gone on to prove him to be the Messiah, by his resurrection from the dead, he makes this conclusion, v. 38, 39. "Be it known unto you, therefore, men and brethren, that through this man is preached unto you forgiveness of sins; and by him all who believe are justified from all things, from which they could not be justified by the law of Moses." This is in this chapter called "the Word of God," over and over again: compare v. 42, with 44, 46, 48, 49, and chap. xii. v. 24.

Acts xvii. 2—4. At Thessalonica, "Paul, as his manner was, went into the synagogue, and three sabbath days reasoned with the jews out of the scriptures; opening and alleging, that the Messiah must needs have suffered, and risen again from the dead: and that this Jesus, whom I preach unto you, is the Messiah. And some of them believed, and consorted with Paul and Silas: but the jews which believed not, set the city in an uproar." Can there be any thing plainer, than that the assenting to this proposition, that Jesus was the Messiah, was that which distinguished the believers from the unbelievers? For this was that alone, which, three sabbaths, Paul endeavoured to convince them of, as the text tells us in direct words.

From thence he went to Berœa, and preached the same thing: and the Berœans are commended, v. 11, for searching the scriptures, whether those things, i. e. which he had said, v. 2, 3, concerning Jesus's being the Messiah, were true or no.

The same doctrine we find him preaching at Corinth, Acts xviii. 4—6. "And he reasoned in the synagogue every sabbath, and persuaded the jews and the Greeks. And when Silas and Timotheus were come from Macedonia, Paul was pressed in spirit, and testified to the jews, that Jesus was the Messiah. And when they opposed themselves, and blasphemed, he shook his raiment, and said unto them, Your blood be upon your own heads, I am clean; from henceforth I will go unto the Greeks."

Upon the like occasion he tells the jews at Antioch, Acts xiii. 46, "It was necessary that the word of God should first have been spoken to you; but seeing you put it off from you, we turn to the gentiles." 'Tis plain here, St. Paul's charging their blood on their own heads, is for opposing this single truth, that Jesus was the Messiah; that salvation or perdition depends upon believing or rejecting this one proposition. I mean, this is all that is required to be believed by those who acknowledge but one eternal and invisible God, the maker of heaven and earth, as the jews did. For that there is something more required to salvation, besides believing, we shall see hereafter. In the mean time, it is fit here on this occasion to take notice, that though the apostles in their preaching to the jews, and the devout, (as we translate the word σε[Editor: illegible character]όμενοι, who were proselytes of the gate, and the worshippers of one eternal and invisible God,) said nothing of the believing in this one true God, the maker of heaven and earth; because it was needless to press this to those who believed and professed it already (for to such, 'tis plain, were most of their discourses hitherto.) Yet when they had to do with idolatrous heathens, who were not yet come to the knowledge of the one only true God; they began with that, as necessary to be believed; it being the foundation on which the other was built, and without which it could signify nothing.

Thus Paul speaking to the idolatrous Lystrians, who would have sacrificed to him and Barnabas, says, Acts xiv. 15, "We preach unto you, that ye should turn from these vanities unto the living God, who made heaven and earth, and the sea, and all things that are therein: who in times past suffered all nations to walk in their own ways. Nevertheless he left not himself without witness, in that he did good, and gave us rain from heaven, and fruitful seasons, filling our hearts with food and gladness."

Thus also he proceeded with the idolatrous Athenians, Acts xvii. telling them, upon occasion of the altar, dedicated to the unknown God, "whom you ignorantly worship, him declare I unto you. God who made the world, and all things therein, seeing that he is Lord of heaven and earth, dwelleth not in temples made with hands.—Forasmuch then as we are the offspring of God, we ought not to think that the Godhead is like unto gold, or silver, or stone, graven by art, or man's device. And the times of this ignorance God winked at; but now commandeth all men every-where to repent; because he hath appointed a day in which he will judge the world in righteousness, by that man whom he hath ordained: whereof he hath given assurance unto all men, in that he hath raised him from the dead." So that we see, where any thing more was necessary to be proposed to be believed, as there was to the heathen idolaters, there the apostles were careful not to omit it.

Acts xviii. 4, "Paul at Corinth reasoned in the synagogue every sabbath-day, and testified to the jews, that Jesus was the Messiah." Ver. 11, "And he continued there a year and six months, teaching the word of God amongst them;" i. e. The good news, that Jesus was the Messiah; as we have already shown is meant by "the Word of God."

Apollos, another preacher of the gospel, when he was instructed in the way of God more perfectly, what did he teach but this same doctrine? As we may see in this account of him, Acts xviii. 27. That, "when he was come into Achaia, he helped the brethren much, who had believed through grace. For he mightily convinced the jews, and that publicly, showing by the scriptures that Jesus was the Messiah."

St. Paul, in the account he gives of himself before Festus and Agrippa, professes this alone to be the doctrine he taught after his conversion: for, says he, Acts xxvi. 22, "Having obtained help of God, I continue unto this day, witnessing both to small and great, saying none other things than those which the prophets and Moses did say should come: that the Messiah should suffer, and that he should be the first that should rise from the dead, and should show light unto the people, and to the gentiles." Which was no more than to prove that Jesus was the Messiah. This is that, which, as we have above observed, is called the Word of God; Acts xi. 1. compared with the foregoing chapter, from v. 34. to the end. And xiii. 42. compared with 44, 46, 48, 49, and xvii. 13. compared with v. 11, 13. It is also called, "the Word of the Gospel," Acts xv. 7. And this is that Word of God, and that Gospel, which, wherever their discourses are set down, we find the apostles preached; and was that faith, which made both jews and gentiles believers and members of the church of Christ; purifying their hearts, Acts xv. 9, and carrying with it remission of sins, Acts x. 43. So that all that was to be believed for justification, was no more but this single proposition, that "Jesus of Nazareth was the Christ, or the Messiah." All, I say, that was to be believed for justification: for that it was not all that was required to be done for justification, we shall see hereafter.

Though we have seen above from what our Saviour has pronounced himself, John iii. 36, "that he that believeth on the Son hath everlasting life; and he that believeth not the Son, shall not see life, but the wrath of God abideth on him;" and are taught from John iv. 39, compared with v. 42, that believing on him, is believing that he is the Messiah, the Saviour of the world; and the confession made by St. Peter, Matt. xvi. 16, that he is "the Messiah, the Son of the living God," being the rock, on which our Saviour has promised to build his church; though this I say, and what else we have already taken notice of, be enough to convince us what it is we are in the gospel required to believe to eternal life, without adding what we have observed from the preaching of the apostles; yet it may not be amiss, for the farther clearing this matter, to observe what the evangelists deliver concerning the same thing, though in different words; which, therefore, perhaps, are not so generally taken notice of to this purpose.

We have above observed, from the words of Andrew and Philip compared, that "the Messiah, and him of whom Moses in the law and the prophets did write," signify the same thing. We shall now consider that place, John i. a little farther. Ver. 41, "Andrew says to Simon, we have found the Messiah." Philip, on the same occasion, v. 45, says to Nathanael, "we have found him of whom Moses in the law and the prophets did write, Jesus of Nazareth, the son of Joseph." Nathanael, who disbelieved this, when, upon Christ's speaking to him, he was convinced of it, declares his assent to it in these words: "Rabbi, thou art the Son of God, thou art the king of Israel." From which it is evident, that to believe him to be "Him of whom Moses and the prophets did write," or to be "the Son of God," or to be "the king of Israel," was in effect the same as to believe him to be the Messiah: and an assent to that, was what our Saviour received for believing. For, upon Nathanael's making a confession in these words, "Thou art the Son of God, thou art the king of Israel, Jesus answered and said to him, Because I said to thee I saw thee under the fig-tree, dost thou believe? Thou shalt see greater things than these," ver. 51. I desire any one to read the latter part of the first of John, from ver. 25, with attention, and tell me, whether it be not plain, that this phrase, The Son of God, is an expression used for the Messiah. To which let him add Martha's declaration of her faith, John xi. 27, in these words: "I believe that thou art the Messiah, the Son of God, who should come into the world;" and that passage of St. John xx. 31, "That ye might believe that Jesus is the Messiah, the Son of God; and that, believing, ye might have life through his name:" and then tell me whether he can doubt that Messiah, the Son of God, were synonymous terms, at that time, amongst the jews.

The prophecy of Daniel, chap. ix. when he is called "Messiah the Prince;" and the mention of his government and kingdom, and the deliverance by him, in Isaiah, Daniel, and other prophecies, understood of the Messiah; were so well known to the jews, and had so raised their hopes of him about this time, which, by their account, was to be the time of his coming, to restore the kingdom of Israel; that Herod no sooner heard of the magi's inquiry after "Him that was born king of the jews," Matt. ii. but he forthwith "demanded of the chief priests and scribes, where the Messiah should be born," ver. 4. Not doubting but, if there were any king born to the jews, it was the Messiah: whose coming was now the general expectation, as appears, Luke iii. 15, "The people being in expectation, and all men musing in their hearts, of John, whether he were the Messiah or not." And when the priests and levites sent to ask him who he was; he, understanding their meaning, answers, John i. 20, "That he was not the Messiah;" but he bears witness, that Jesus "is the Son of God." i. e. the Messiah, ver. 34.

This looking for the Messiah, at this time, we see also in Simeon; who is said to be "waiting for the consolation of Israel," Luke ii. 21. And having the child Jesus in his arms, he says he had "seen the salvation of the Lord," ver. 30. And, "Anna coming at the same instant into the temple, she gave thanks also unto the Lord, and spake of him to all them that looked for redemption in Israel," ver. 38. And of Joseph of Arimathea, it is said, Mark xv. 43, That "he also expected the kingdom of God:" by all which was meant the coming of the Messiah; and Luke xix. 11, it is said, "They thought that the kingdom of God should immediately appear."

This being premised, let us see what it was that John the Baptist preached, when he first entered upon his ministry. That St. Matthew tells us, chap. iii. 1, 2, "In those days came John the Baptist preaching in the wilderness of Judea, saying, repent; for the kingdom of heaven is at hand." This was a declaration of the coming of the Messiah: the kingdom of heaven, and the kingdom of God, being the same, as is clear out of several places of the evangelists; and both signifying the kingdom of the Messiah. The profession which John the Baptist made, when sent to the jews, John i. 19, was, that "he was not the Messiah;" but that Jesus was. This will appear to any one, who will compare ver. 26—34, with John iii. 27, 30. The jews being very inquisitive to know, whether John were the Messiah; he positively denies it; but tells them, he was only his forerunner; and that there stood one amongst them, who would follow him, whose shoe-latchet he was not worthy to untie. The next day, seeing Jesus, he says, he was the man; and that his own baptizing in water was only that Jesus might be manifested to the world; and that he knew him not, till he saw the Holy Ghost descend upon him: he that sent him to baptize, having told him, that he on whom he should see the Spirit descend, and rest upon, he it was that should baptize with the Holy Ghost; and that therefore he witnessed, that "this was the Son of God," ver. 34, i. e. the Messiah; and, chap. iii. 26, &c. they come to John the Baptist, and tell him, that Jesus baptized, and that all men went to him. John answers, He has his authority from heaven; you know I never said, I was the Messiah, but that I was sent before him. He must increase, but I must decrease; for God hath sent him, and he speaks the words of God; and God hath given all things into the hands of his Son, "And he that believes on the Son, hath eternal life;" the same doctrine, and nothing else but what was preached by the apostles afterwards: as we have seen all through the Acts. v. g. that Jesus was the Messiah. And thus it was, that John bears witness of our Saviour, as Jesus himself says, John v. 33.

This also was the declaration given of him at his baptism, by a voice from heaven: "This is my beloved Son in whom I am well pleased." Matt. iii. 17. Which was a declaration of him to be the Messiah, the Son of God being (as we have showed) understood to signify the Messiah. To which we may add the first mention of him after his conception, in the words of the angel to Joseph, Matt. i. 21. "Thou shalt call his name Jesus," or Saviour; "for he shall save his people from their sins." It was a received doctrine in the jewish nation, that at the coming of the Messiah, all their sins should be forgiven them. These words, therefore, of the angel, we may look upon as a declaration, that Jesus was the Messiah; whereof these words, "his people," are a farther mark: which suppose him to have a people, and consequently to be a king.

After his baptism, Jesus himself enters upon his ministry. But, before we examine what it was he proposed to be believed, we must observe, that there is a threefold declaration of the Messiah.

1. By miracles. The spirit of prophecy had now for many ages forsaken the jews; and, though their commonwealth were not quite dissolved, but that they lived under their own laws, yet they were under a foreign dominion, subject to the Romans. In this state their account of the time being up, they were in expectation of the Messiah, and of deliverance by him in a kingdom he was to set up, according to their ancient prophecies of him: which gave them hopes of an extraordinary man yet to come from God, who, with an extraordinary and divine power, and miracles, should evidence his mission, and work their deliverance. And, of any such extraordinary person, who should have the power of doing miracles, they had no other expectation, but only of their Messiah. One great prophet and worker of miracles, and only one more, they expected; who was to be the Messiah. And therefore we see the people justified their believing in him, i. e. their believing him to be the Messiah, because of the miracles he did; John vii. 41. "And many of the people believed in him, and said, When the Messiah cometh, will he do more miracles, than this man hath done?" And when the jews, at the feast of dedication, John x. 24, 25, coming about him, said unto him, "How long dost thou make us doubt? If thou be the Messiah, tell us plainly; Jesus answered them, I told you, and ye believed not; the works that I do in my Father's name bear witness of me." And, John v. 36, he says, "I have a greater witness than that of John; for the works, which the Father hath given me to do, the same works that I do, bear witness of me, that the Father hath sent me." Where, by the way, we may observe, that his being "sent by the Father," is but another way of expressing the Messiah; which is evident from

this place here, John v. compared with that of John x. last quoted. For there he says, that his works bear witness of him: And what was that witness? viz. That he was "the Messiah." Here again he says, that his works bear witness of him: And what is that witness? viz. "That the Father sent him." By which we are taught, that to be sent by the Father, and to be the Messiah, was the same thing, in his way of declaring himself. And accordingly we find, John iv. 53, and xi. 45, and elsewhere, many hearkened and assented to his testimony, and believed on him, seeing the things that he did.

2. Another way of declaring the coming of the Messiah, was by phrases and circumlocutions, that did signify or intimate his coming; though not in direct words pointing out the person. The most usual of these were, "The kingdom of God, and of heaven;" because it was that which was often spoken of the Messiah, in the Old Testament, in very plain words: and a kingdom was that which the jews most looked after and wished for. In that known place, Isa. ix. "The government shall be upon his shoulders; he shall be called the Prince of peace: of the increase of his government and peace there shall be no end; upon the throne of David, and upon his kingdom, to order it, and to establish it with judgment, and with justice, from henceforth even for ever." Micah v. 2, "But thou, Bethlehem Ephratah, though thou be little among the thousands of Judah, yet out of thee shall he come forth unto me, that is to be the Ruler in Israel." And Daniel, besides that he calls him "Messiah the Prince," chap. ix. 25, in the account of his vision "of the Son of man," chap. vii. 13, 14, says, "There was given him dominion, glory, and a kingdom, that all people, nations, and languages should serve him: his dominion is an everlasting dominion, which shall not pass away; and his kingdom that which shall not be destroyed." So that the kingdom of God, and the kingdom of heaven, were common phrases amongst the jews, to signify the times of the Messiah. Luke xiv. 15, "One of the jews that sat at meat with him, said unto him, Blessed is he that shall eat bread in the kingdom of God." Chap. xvii. 20, The pharisees demanded, "when the kingdom of God should come?" And St. John Baptist "came, saying, Repent; for the kingdom of heaven is at hand;" a phrase he would not have used in preaching, had it not been understood.

There are other expressions that signified the Messiah, and his coming, which we shall take notice of, as they come in our way.

3. By plain and direct words, declaring the doctrine of the Messiah, speaking out that Jesus was he; as we see the apostles did, when they went about preaching the gospel, after our Saviour's resurrection. This was the open clear way, and that which one would think the Messiah himself, when he came, should have taken; especially, if it were of that moment, that upon men's believing him to be the Messiah depended the forgiveness of their sins. And yet we see, that our Saviour did not: but on the contrary, for the most part, made no other discovery of himself, at least in Judea, and at the beginning of his ministry, but in the two former ways, which were more obscure: not declaring himself to be the Messiah, any otherwise than as it might be gathered from the miracles he did, and the conformity of his life and actions with the prophecies of the Old Testament concerning him: and from some general discourses of the kingdom of the Messiah being come, under the name of the "kingdom of God, and of heaven." Nay, so far was he from publicly owning himself to be the Messiah, that he forbid the doing of it: Mark viii. 27—30. "He asked his disciples, Whom do men say that I am? And they answered, John the Baptist; but some say Elias; and others, one of the prophets." (So that it is evident, that even those, who

believed him an extraordinary person, knew not yet who he was, or that he gave himself out for the Messiah; though this was in the third year of his ministry, and not a year before his death.) "And he saith unto them, But whom say ye that I am? And Peter answered and said unto him, Thou art the Messiah. And he charged them, that they should tell no man of him." Luke iv. 41. "And devils came out of many, crying, Thou art the Messiah, the Son of God: and he, rebuking them, suffered them not to speak, that they knew him to be the Messiah." Mark iii. 11, 12. "Unclean spirits, when they saw him, fell down before him, and cried, saying, Thou art the Son of God: and he straitly charged them, that they should not make him known." Here again we may observe, from the comparing of the two texts, that "Thou art the Son of God," or, "Thou art the Messiah," were indifferently used for the same thing. But to return to the matter in hand.

This concealment of himself will seem strange, in one who was come to bring light into the world, and was to suffer death for the testimony of the truth. This reservedness will be thought to look, as if he had a mind to conceal himself, and not to be known to the world for the Messiah, nor to be believed on as such. But we shall be of another mind, and conclude this proceeding of his according to divine wisdom, and suited to a fuller manifestation and evidence of his being the Messiah; when we consider that he was to fill out the time foretold of his ministry; and after a life illustrious in miracles and good works, attended with humility, meekness, patience, and sufferings, and every way conformable to the prophecies of him; should be led as a sheep to the slaughter, and with all quiet and submission be brought to the cross, though there were no guilt, nor fault found in him. This could not have been, if, as soon as he appeared in public, and began to preach, he had presently professed himself to have been the Messiah; the king that owned that kingdom, he published to be at hand. For the sanhedrim would then have laid hold on it, to have got him into their power, and thereby have taken away his life; at least they would have disturbed his ministry, and hindered the work he was about. That this made him cautious, and avoid, as much as he could, the occasions of provoking them and falling into their hands, is plain from John vii. 1. "After these things Jesus walked in Galilee;" out of the way of the chief priests and rulers; "for he would not walk in Jewry, because the jews sought to kill him." Thus, making good what he foretold them at Jerusalem, when, at the first passover after his beginning to preach the gospel, upon his curing the man at the pool of Bethesda, they sought to kill him, John v. 16, "Ye have not," says he, ver. 38, "his word abiding amongst you; for whom he hath sent, him ye believe not." This was spoken more particularly to the jews of Jerusalem, who were the forward men, zealous to take away his life: and it imports, that, because of their unbelief and opposition to him, the word of God, i. e. the preaching of the kingdom of the Messiah, which is often called "the word of God," did not stay amongst them, he could not stay amongst them, preach and explain to them the kingdom of the Messiah.

That the word of God, here, signifies "the word of God," that should make Jesus known to them to be the Messiah, is evident from the context: and this meaning of this place is made good by the event. For, after this, we hear no more of Jesus at Jerusalem, till the pentecost come twelvemonth; though it is not to be doubted, but that he was there the next passover, and other feasts between; but privately. And now at Jerusalem, at the feast of pentecost, near fifteen months after, he says little of any thing, and not a word of the kingdom of heaven being come, or at hand; nor did he any miracle there. And returning to Jerusalem at the feast of tabernacles, it is plain, that from this time 'till then, which was a year and a half, he had not taught them at Jerusalem.

For, 1. it is said, John vii. 2, 15, That, he teaching in the temple at the feast of tabernacles, "the jews marvelled, saying, How knoweth this man letters, having never learned?" A sign they had not been used to his preaching: for, if they had, they would not now have marvelled.

2. Ver. 19, He says thus to them: "Did not Moses give you the law, and yet none of you keep the law? Why go ye about to kill me? One work," or miracle, "I did here amongst you, and ye all marvel. Moses therefore gave unto you circumcision, and ye on the sabbath-day circumcise a man: if a man on the sabbath-day receive circumcision, that the law of Moses should not be broken, are ye angry with me, because I have made a man every way whole on the sabbath-day?" Which is a direct defence of what he did at Jerusalem, a year and a half before the work he here speaks of. We find he had not preached to them there, from that time to this; but had made good what he had told them, ver. 38, "Ye have not the word of God remaining among you, because whom he hath sent ye believe not." Whereby, I think, he signifies his not staying, and being frequent amongst them at Jerusalem, preaching the gospel of the kingdom; because their great unbelief, opposition, and malice to him, would not permit it.

This was manifestly so in fact: for the first miracle he did at Jerusalem, which was at the second passover after his baptism, brought him in danger of his life. Hereupon we find he forbore preaching again there, 'till the feast of tabernacles, immediately preceding his last passover: so that 'till the half a year before his passion, he did but one miracle, and preached but once publicly at Jerusalem. These trials he made there; but found their unbelief such, that if he had staid and persisted to preach the good tidings of the kingdom, and to show himself by miracles among them, he could not have had time and freedom to do those works which his Father had given him to finish, as he says, ver. 36, of this fifth of St. John.

When, upon the curing of the withered hand on the sabbath-day, "The pharisees took counsel with the herodians, how they might destroy him, Jesus withdrew himself, with his disciples, to the sea: and a great multitude from Galilee followed him, and from Judea, and from Jerusalem, and from Idumea, and from beyond Jordan, and they about Tyre and Sidon, a great multitude; when they had heard what great things he did, came unto him, and he healed them all, and charged them, that they should not make him known: that it might be fulfilled which was spoken by the prophet Isaiah, saying, Behold, my servant, whom I have chosen; my beloved, in whom my soul is well pleased: I will put my spirit upon him, and he shall show judgment to the gentiles. He shall not strive, nor cry, neither shall any man hear his voice in the streets." Matt. xii. Mark iii.

And, John xi. 47, upon the news of our Saviour's raising Lazarus from the dead, "The chief priests and pharisees convened the sanhedrim, and said, What do we? For this man does many miracles." Ver. 53, "Then from that day forth they took counsel together for to put him to death." Ver. 54, "Jesus therefore walked no more openly amongst the jews." His miracles had now so much declared him to be the Messiah, that the jews could no longer bear him, nor he trust himself amongst them; "But went thence unto a country near to the wilderness, into a city called Ephraim; and there continued with his disciples." This was but a little before his last passover, as appears by the following words, ver. 55. "And the jews passover was nigh at hand," and he could not, now his miracles had made him so well known, have been secure, the little time that remained, 'till his hour was fully come, if he had not, with his wonted and necessary caution, withdrawn; "And walked no more openly amongst the jews," 'till his time (at the next passover) was fully come; and then again he appeared amongst them openly.

Nor would the Romans have suffered him, if he had gone about preaching, that he was the king whom the jews expected. Such an accusation would have been forwardly brought against him by the jews, if they could have heard it out of his own mouth; and that had been his public doctrine to his followers, which was openly preached by the apostles after his death, when he appeared no more. And of this they were accused, Acts xvii. 5—9. "But the jews, which believed not, moved with envy, took unto them certain lewd fellows of the baser sort, and gathered a company, and set all the city in an uproar, and assaulted the house of Jason, and sought to bring them out to the people. And when they found them [Paul and Silas] not, they drew Jason, and certain brethren, unto the rulers of the city, crying, These that have turned the world upside down, are come hither also; whom Jason hath received: and these all do contrary to the decrees of Cæsar, saying, That there is another king, one Jesus. And they troubled the people, and the rulers of the city, when they heard these things: and when they had taken security of Jason and the other, they let them go."

Though the magistrates of the world had no great regard to the talk of a king who had suffered death, and appeared no longer any where; yet, if our Saviour had openly declared this of himself in his life time, with a train of disciples and followers every where owning and crying him up for their king; the Roman governors of Judea could not have forborne to have taken notice of it, and have made use of their force against him. This the jews were not mistaken in; and therefore made use of it as the strongest accusation, and likeliest to prevail with Pilate against him, for the taking away his life; it being treason, and an unpardonable offence, which could not escape death from a Roman deputy, without the forfeiture of his own life. Thus then they accuse him to Pilate, Luke xxiii. 2. "We found this fellow perverting the nation, forbidding to give tribute to Cæsar, saying, that he himself is a king;" or rather "the Messiah, the King."

Our Saviour, indeed, now that his time was come, (and he in custody, and forsaken of all the world, and so out of all danger of raising any sedition or disturbance,) owns himself to Pilate to be a king; after first having told Pilate, John xviii. 36, "That his kingdom was not of this world;" and, for a kingdom in another world, Pilate knew that his master at Rome concerned not himself. But had there been any the least appearance of truth in the allegations of the jews, that he had perverted the nation, forbidding to pay tribute to Cæsar, or drawing the people after him, as their king; Pilate would not so readily have pronounced him innocent. But we see what he said to his accusers, Luke xxiii. 13, 14. "Pilate, when he had called together the chief priests and the rulers of the people, said unto them, You have brought this man unto me as one that perverteth the people; and behold, I, having examined him before you, have found no fault in this man, touching those things whereof you accuse him: no, nor yet Herod, for I sent you to him; and, lo, nothing worthy of death is done by him." And therefore, finding a man of that mean condition, and innocent life, (no mover of seditions, or disturber of the public peace) without a friend or a follower, he would have dismissed him, as a king of no consequence; as an innocent man, falsely and maliciously accused by the jews.

How necessary this caution was in our Saviour, to say or do nothing that might justly offend, or render him suspected to the Roman governor: and how glad the jews would have been to have had any such thing against him, we may see, Luke xx. 20. The chief priests and the scribes "watched him, and sent forth spies, who should feign themselves just men, that might take hold of his words, that so they might deliver him unto the power and authority of the governor." And the very thing wherein they hoped to entrap him in this place, was paying tribute to Cæsar; which they afterwards falsely accused him of. And what would they have done, if he had before them professed himself to have been the Messiah, their King and deliverer?

And here we may observe the wonderful providence of God, who had so ordered the state of the jews, at the time when his son was to come into the world, that though neither their civil constitution nor religious worship were dissolved, yet the power of life and death was taken from them; whereby he had an opportunity to publish "the kingdom of the Messiah;" that is, his own royalty, under the name of "the kingdom of God, and of heaven;" which the jews well enough understood, and would certainly have put him to death for, had the power been in their own hands. But this being no matter of accusation to the Romans, hindered him not from speaking of the "kingdom of heaven," as he did, sometimes in reference to his appearing in the world, and being believed on by particular persons; sometimes in reference to the power should be given him by the Father at his resurrection; and sometimes in reference to his coming to judge the world at the last day, in the full glory and completion of his kingdom. These were ways of declaring himself, which the jews could lay no hold on, to bring him in danger with Pontius Pilate, and get him seized and put to death.

Another reason there was, that hindered him as much as the former, from professing himself, in express words, to be the Messiah; and that was, that the whole nation of the jews, expecting at this time their Messiah, and deliverance, by him, from the subjection they were in to a foreign yoke, the body of the people would certainly, upon his declaring himself to be the Messiah, their king, have rose up in rebellion, and set him at the head of them. And indeed, the miracles that he did, so much disposed them to think him to be the Messiah, that, though shrouded under the obscurity of a mean condition, and a very private simple life; though he passed for a Galilean (his birth at Bethlehem being then concealed), and assumed not to himself any power or authority, or so much as the name of the Messiah; yet he could hardly avoid being set up by a tumult, and proclaimed their king. So John tells us, chap. vi. 14, 15, "Then those men, when they had seen the miracles that Jesus did, said, This is of a truth that prophet that should come into the world. When therefore Jesus perceived that they would come to take him by force to make him king, he departed again into a mountain, himself alone." This was upon his feeding of five thousand with five barley loaves and two fishes. So hard was it for him, doing those miracles which were necessary to testify his mission, and which often drew great multitudes after him, Matt. iv. 25, to keep the heady and hasty multitude from such disorder, as would have involved him in it; and have disturbed the course, and cut short the time of his ministry; and drawn on him the reputation and death of a turbulent, seditious malefactor; contrary to the design of his coming, which was, to be offered up a lamb blameless, and void of offence; his innocence appearing to all the world, even to him that delivered him up to be crucified. This it would have been impossible to have avoided, if, in his preaching every-where, he had openly assumed to himself the title of their Messiah; which was all was wanting to set the people in a flame; who drawn by his miracles, and the hopes of finding a Deliverer in so extraordinary a man, followed him in great numbers. We read every-where of multitudes, and in Luke xii. 1, of myriads that were gathered about him. This conflux of people, thus disposed, would not have failed, upon his declaring himself to be the Messiah, to have made a commotion, and with force set him up for their King. It is plain, therefore, from these two reasons, why (though he came to preach the gospel, and convert the world to a belief of his being the Messiah; and though he says so much of his kingdom, under the title of the kingdom of God, and the kingdom of heaven) he yet makes it not his business to persuade them, that he himself is the Messiah, nor does, in his public preaching, declare himself to be him. He inculcates to the people, on all occasions, that the kingdom of God is come: he shows the way of admittance into this kingdom, viz. repentance and baptism; and teaches the laws of it, viz. good life, according to the strictest rules of virtue and morality. But who the King was of this kingdom, he leaves to his miracles to point out, to those who would consider what he did, and make the right use of it now; or to witness to those who should hearken to the apostles hereafter when they preached it in plain words, and called upon them to believe it, after his resurrection, when there should be no longer room to fear, that it should cause any disturbance in civil societies, and the governments of the world. But he could not declare himself to be the Messiah, without manifest danger of tumult and sedition: and the miracles he did declared it so much, that he was fain often to hide himself, and withdraw from the concourse of the people. The leper that he cured, Mark i, though forbid to say any thing, yet "blazed it so abroad, that Jesus could no more openly enter into the city, but was without in desert places," living in retirement, as appears from Luke v. 16, and there "they came to him from every quarter." And thus he did more than once.

This being premised, let us take a view of the promulgation of the gospel by our Saviour himself, and see what it was he taught the world, and required men to believe.

The first beginning of his ministry, whereby he showed himself, seems to be at Cana in Galilee, soon after his baptism; where he turned water into wine: of which St. John, chap. ii. 11, says thus: "This beginning of miracles Jesus made, and manifested his glory, and his disciples believed in him." His disciples here believed in him, but we hear not of any other preaching to them, but by this miracle, whereby he "manifested his glory," i. e. of being the Messiah, the Prince. So Nathanael, without any other preaching, but only our Saviour's discovering to him, that he knew him after an extraordinary manner, presently acknowledges him to be the Messiah; crying, "Rabbi, thou art the Son of God; thou art the King of Israel."

From hence, staying a few days at Capernaum, he goes to Jerusalem, to the passover, and there he drives the traders out of the temple, John ii. 12—15, saying, "Make not my Father's house a house of merchandize." Where we see he uses a phrase, which, by interpretation, signifies that he was the "Son of God," though at that time unregarded. Ver. 16, Hereupon the jews demand, "What sign dost thou show us, since thou doest these things?" Jesus answered, "Destroy ye this temple, and in three days I will raise it again." This is an instance of what way Jesus took to declare himself: for it is plain, by their reply, the jews understood him not, nor his disciples neither; for it is said, ver. 22, "When, therefore, he was risen from the dead, his disciples remembered, that he said this to them: and they believed the scripture, and the saying of Jesus to them."

This, therefore, we may look on in the beginning, as a pattern of Christ's preaching, and showing himself to the jews, which he generally followed afterwards; viz. such a manifestation of himself, as every one at present could not understand; but yet carried such an evidence with it, to those who were well disposed now, or would reflect on it when the whole course of his ministry was over, as was sufficient clearly to convince them that he was the Messiah.

The reason of this method used by our Saviour, the scripture gives us here, at this his first appearing in public, after his entrance upon his ministry, to be a rule and light to us in the whole course of it: for the next verse taking notice, that many believed on him, "because of his miracles," (which was all the preaching they had,) it is said, ver. 24, "But Jesus did not commit himself unto them, because he knew all men;" i. e. he declared not himself so openly to be the Messiah, their King, as to put himself into the power of the jews, by laying himself open to their malice; who, he knew, would be so ready to lay hold on it to accuse him; for, as the next verse 25, shows, he knew well enough what was in them. We may here further observe, that "believing in his name" signifies believing him to be the Messiah. Ver. 22, tells us, That "many at the passover believed in his name, when they saw the miracles that he did." What other faith could these miracles produce in them who saw them, but that this was he of whom the scripture spoke, who was to be their Deliverer?

Whilst he was now at Jerusalem, Nicodemus, a ruler of the jews, comes to him, John iii. 1—21, to whom he preaches eternal life by faith in the Messiah, ver. 15 and 17, but in general terms, without naming himself to be that Messiah, though his whole discourse tends to it. This is all we hear of our Saviour the first year of his ministry, but only his baptism, fasting, and temptation in the beginning of it, and spending the rest of it after the passover, in Judea with his disciples, baptizing there. But "when he knew that the pharisees reported, that he made and baptized more disciples than John, he left Judea," and got out of their way again into Galilee, John iv. 1, 3.

In his way back, by the well of Sichar, he discourses with the Samaritan woman; and after having opened to her the true and spiritual worship which was at hand, which the woman presently understands of the times of the Messiah, who was then looked for; thus she answers, ver. 25, "I know that the Messiah cometh: when he is come, he will tell us all things." Whereupon our Saviour, though we hear no such thing from him in Jerusalem or Judea, or to Nicodemus; yet here, to this Samaritan woman, he in plain and direct words owns and declares, that he himself, who talked with her, was the Messiah, ver. 26.

This would seem very strange, that he should be more free and open to a Samaritan, than he was to the jews, were not the reason plain, from what we have observed above. He was now out of Judea,, among a people with whom the jews had no commerce; ver. 9, who were not disposed, out of envy, as the jews were, to seek his life, or to accuse him to the Roman governor, or to make an insurrection, to set a jew up for their King. What the consequence was of his discourse with this Samaritan woman, we have an account, ver. 28, 39—42. "She left her water-pot, and went her way into the city, and saith to the men, Come, see a man who told me all things that ever I did: Is not this the Messiah? And many of the Samaritans of that city believed on him for the saying of the woman, which testified, He told me all that ever I did. So when the Samaritans were come unto him, they besought him, that he would tarry with them: and he abode there two days. And many more believed because of his own word; and said unto the woman, Now we believe not because of thy saying: for we have heard him ourselves; and we know," (i.e. are fully persuaded) "that this is indeed the Messiah, the Saviour of the world." By comparing ver. 39, with 41 and 42, it is plain, that "believing on him" signifies no more than believing him to be the Messiah.

From Sichar Jesus goes to Nazareth, the place he was bred up in; and there reading in the synagogue a prophecy concerning the Messiah, out of the lxi. of Isaiah, he tells them, Luke iv. 21, "This day is this scripture fulfilled in your ears."

But being in danger of his life at Nazareth, he leaves it for Capernaum: and then, as St. Matthew informs us, chap. iv. 17, "He began to preach and say, Repent; for the kingdom of heaven is at hand." Or, as St. Mark has it, chap. i. 14, 15, "Preaching the gospel of the kingdom of God, and saying, The time is fulfilled, and the kingdom of God is at hand; repent ye, and believe the gospel;" i. e. believe this good news. This removing to Capernaum, and seating himself there in the borders of Zabulon and Naphtali, was, as St. Matthew observes, chap. iv. 13—16, that a prophecy of Isaiah might be fulfilled. Thus the actions and circumstances of his life answered the prophecies, and declared him to be the Messiah. And by what St. Mark says in this place, it is manifest, that the gospel which he preached and required them to believe, was no other but the good tidings of the coming of the Messiah, and of his kingdom, the time being now fulfilled.

In his way to Capernaum, being come to Cana, a nobleman of Capernaum came to him, ver. 47, "And besought him that he would come down and heal his son; for he was at the point of death." Ver. 48, "Then said Jesus unto him, Except ye see signs and wonders, ye will not believe." Then he returning homewards, and finding that his son began to "mend at the same hour which Jesus said unto him, Thy son liveth; he himself believed, and his whole house," ver. 53.

Here this nobleman is by the apostles pronounced to be a believer. And what does he believe? Even that which Jesus complains, ver. 48, "they would not believe, except they saw signs and wonders; which could be nothing but what those of Samaria in the same chapter believed, viz. that he was the Messiah. For we no-where in the gospel hear of any thing else, that had been proposed to be believed by them.

Having done miracles, and cured all their sick at Capernaum, he says, "Let us go to the adjoining towns, that I may preach there also; for therefore came I forth," Mark i. 38. Or, as St. Luke has it, chap. iv. 43, he tells the multitude, who would have kept him, that he might not go from them, "I must evangelize," or tell the good tidings of "the kingdom of God to other cities also; for therefore am I sent." And St. Matthew, chap. iv. 23, tells us how he executed this commission he was sent on: "And Jesus went about all Galilee, teaching in their synagogues, and preaching the gospel of the kingdom, and curing all diseases." This then was what he was sent to preach every-where, viz. the gospel of the kingdom of the Messiah; and by the miracles and good he did he let them know who was the Messiah.

Hence he goes up to Jerusalem, to the second passover, since the beginning of his ministry. And here, discoursing to the jews, who sought to kill him upon occasion of the man whom he had cured carrying his bed on the sabbath-day, and for making God his Father, he tells them that he wrought these things by the power of God, and that he shall do greater things; for that the dead shall, at his summons, be raised; and that he, by a power committed to him from his Father, shall judge them; and that he is sent by his Father, and that whoever shall hear his word, and believe in him that sent him, has eternal life. This though a clear description of the Messiah, yet we may observe, that here, to the angry jews, who sought to kill him, he says not a word of his kingdom, nor so much as names the Messiah; but yet that he is the Son of God, and sent from God, he refers them to the testimony of John the Baptist; to the testimony of his own miracles, and of God himself in the voice from heaven, and of the scriptures, and of Moses. He leaves them to learn from these the truth they were to believe, viz. that he was the Messiah sent from God. This you may read more at large, John v. 1—47.

The next place where we find him preaching, was on the mount, Matt. v. and Luke vi. This is by much the longest sermon we have of his, any-where; and, in all likelihood, to the greatest auditory: for it appears to have been to the people gathered to him from Galilee, and Judea, and Jerusalem, and from beyond Jordan, and that came out of Idumea, and from Tyre and Sidon, mentioned Mark iii. 7, 8. and Luke vi. 17. But in this whole sermon of his, we do not find one word of believing, and therefore no mention of the Messiah, or any intimation to the people who himself was. The reason whereof we may gather from Matt. xii. 16, where "Christ forbids them to make him known;" which supposes them to know already who he was. For that this 12th chapter of St. Matthew ought to precede the sermon in the mount, is plain, by comparing it with Mark ii. beginning at ver. 13, to Mark iii. 8, and comparing those chapters of St. Mark with Luke vi. And I desire my reader, once for all, here to take notice, that I have all along observed the order of time in our Saviour's preaching, and have not, as I think, passed by any of his discourses. In this sermon, our Saviour only teaches them what were the laws of his kingdom, and what they must do who were admitted into it, of which I shall have occasion to speak more at large in another place, being at present only inquiring what our Saviour proposed as matter of faith to be believed.

After this, John the Baptist sends to him this message, Luke vii. 19, asking, "Art thou he that should come, or do we expect another?" That is, in short, Art thou the Messiah? And if thou art, why dost thou let me, thy forerunner, languish in prison? Must I expect deliverance from any other? To which Jesus returns this answer, ver. 22, 23, "Tell John what ye have seen and heard; the blind see, the lame walk, the lepers are cleansed, the deaf hear, the dead are raised, to the poor the gospel is preached; and blessed is he who is not offended in me." What it is to be "offended, or scandalized in him," we may see by comparing Matt. xiii. 28, and Mark iv. 17, with Luke viii. 13. For what the two first call "scandalized," the last call "standing off from, or forsaking," i. e. not receiving him as the Messiah (vid. Mark vi. 1—6.) or revolting from him. Here Jesus refers John, as he did the jews before, to the testimony of his miracles, to know who he was; and this was generally his preaching, whereby he declared himself to be the Messiah, who was the only prophet to come, whom the jews had any expectation of; nor did they look for any other person to be sent to them with the power of miracles, but only the Messiah. His miracles, we see by his answer to John the Baptist, he thought a sufficient declaration amongst them, that he was the Messiah. And therefore, upon his curing the possessed of the devil, the dumb, and blind, Matt. xii. the people, who saw the miracles, said, ver. 23, "Is not this the son of David?" As much as to say, Is not this the Messiah? Whereat the pharisees being offended, said, "He cast out devils by Beelzebub." Jesus, showing the falsehood and vanity of their blasphemy, justifies the conclusion the people made from this miracle, saying, ver. 28, That his casting out devils by the Spirit of God, was an evidence that the kingdom of the Messiah was come.

One thing more there was in the miracles done by his disciples, which showed him to be the Messiah; that they were done in his name. "In the name of Jesus of "Nazareth, rise up and walk," says St. Peter to the lame man, whom he cured in the temple, Acts iii. 6. And how far the power of that name reached, they themselves seem to wonder, Luke x. 17. "And the seventy returned again with joy, saying, Lord, even the devils are subject to us in thy name."

From this message from John the Baptist, he takes occasion to tell the people that John was the forerunner of the Messiah; that from the time of John the Baptist the kingdom of the Messiah began; to which time all the prophets and the law pointed, Luke vii. and Matt. xi.

Luke viii. 1, "Afterwards he went through every city and village, preaching and showing the good tidings of the kingdom of God." Here we see as everywhere, what his preaching was, and consequently what was to be believed.

Soon after, he preaches from a boat to the people on the shore. His sermon at large we may read, Matt. xiii. Mark iv. and Luke viii. But this is very observable, that this second sermon of his, here, is quite different from his former in the mount: for that was all so plain and intelligible, that nothing could be more so; whereas this is all so involved in parables, that even the apostles themselves did not understand it. If we inquire into the reason of this, we shall possibly have some light, from the different subjects of these two sermons. There he preached to the people only morality; clearing the precepts of the law from the false glosses which were received in those days, and setting forth th duties of a good life in their full obligation and extent, beyond what the judiciary laws of the Israelites did, or the civil laws of any country could prescribe, or take notice of. But here, in this sermon by the sea-side, he speaks of nothing but the kingdom of the Messiah, which he does all in parables. One reason whereof St. Matthew gives us, chap. xiii. 35, "That it might be fulfilled which was spoken by the prophets," saying, "I will open my mouth in parables, I will utter things that have been kept secret from the foundations of the world." Another reason our Saviour himself gives of it, ver. 11, 12, Because to you is given to know the mysteries of the kingdom of heaven, but to them it is not given. For whosoever hath, to him shall be given, and he shall have more abundantly; but whosoever hath not," i. e. improves not the talents that he hath, "from him shall be taken away even that he hath."

One thing it may not be amiss to observe, that our Saviour here, in the explication of the first of these parables to his apostles, calls the preaching of the kingdom of the Messiah, simply, "The word," and Luke viii. 21, "The word of God:" from whence St. Luke, in the Acts, often mentions it under the name of the "word," and "the word of God," as we have elsewhere observed. To which I shall here add that of Acts viii. 4, "Therefore they that were scattered abroad, went every-where preaching the word;" which word, as we have found by examining what they preached all through their history, was nothing but this, that "Jesus was the Messiah:" I mean, this was all the doctrine they proposed to be believed: for what they taught, as well as our Saviour, contained a great deal more; but that concerned practice, and not belief. And therefore our Saviour says, in the place before quoted, Luke viii. 21, "they are my mother and my brethren, who hear the word of God, and do it:" obeying the law of the Messiah their king being no less required, than their believing that Jesus was the Messiah, the king and deliverer that was promised them.

Matt. ix. 13, we have an account again of this preaching; what it was, and how: "And Jesus went about all the cities and villages, teaching in their synagogues, and preaching the gospel of the kingdom, and healing every sickness and every disease among the people." He acquainted them, that the kingdom of the Messiah was come. and left it to his miracles to instruct and convince them, that he was the Messiah.

Matt. x. when he sent his apostles abroad, their commission to preach we have, ver. 7, 8, in these words: "As ye go, preach saying, The kingdom of heaven is at hand: heal the sick," &c. All that they had to preach was, that the kingdom of the Messiah was come.

Whosoever should not receive them, the messengers of these good tidings, nor hearken to their message, incurred a heavier doom than Sodom and Gomorrah, at the day of judgment, ver. 14, 15. But ver. 32, "Whosoever shall confess me before men, I will confess him before my Father who is in heaven." What this confessing of Christ is, we may see by comparing John xii. 42. with ix. 22. "Nevertheless, among the chief rulers also many believed on him; but because of the pharisees they did not confess him, lest they should be put out of the synagogue. And chap. ix. 22, "These words spake his parents, because they feared the jews; for the jews had agreed already, that if any man did confess that he was the Messiah, he should be put out of the synagogue." By which places it is evident, that to confess him was to confess that he was the Messiah. From which, give me leave to observe also, (what I have cleared from other places, but cannot be too often remarked, because of the different sense has been put upon that phrase) viz. "that believing on, or in him," (for εἰς αὐτὸν is rendered either way by the English translation,) signifies believing that he was the Messiah. For many of the rulers (the text says) "believed on him:" but they durst not confess what they believed, "for fear they should be put out of the synagogue." Now the offence for which it was agreed that any one should be put out of the synagogue, was, if he "did confess, that Jesus was the Messiah." Hence we may have a clear understanding of that passage of St. Paul to the Romans, where he tells them positively, what is the faith he preaches, Rom. x. 8, 9, "That is the word of faith which we preach, that if thou shalt confess with thy mouth the Lord Jesus, and believe in thine heart, that God hath raised him from the dead, thou shalt be saved;" and that also of 1 John iv. 14, 15, "We have seen, and do testify, that the Father sent the Son to be the Saviour of the world: whosoever shall confess, that Jesus is the Son of God, God dwelleth in him, and he in God." Where confessing Jesus to be the Son of God, is the same with confessing him to be the Messiah; those two expressions being understood amongst the jews to signify the same thing, as we have shown already.

How calling him the Son of God, came to signify that he was the Messiah, would not be hard to show. But it is enough, that it appears plainly, that it was so used, and had that import among the jews at that time: which if any one desires to have further evidenced to him, he may add Matt. xxvi. 63. John vi. 69. and xi. 27. and xx. 31. to those places before occasionally taken notice of.

As was the apostles commission, such was their performance; as we read, Luke xi. 6, "They departed and went through the towns, preaching the gospel, and healing every-where." Jesus bid them preach, "saying, The kingdom of heaven is at hand." And St. Luke tells us, they went through the towns preaching the gospel; a word which in Saxon answers well the Greek εὐαγγέλιον, and signifies, as that does, "good news." So that what the inspired writers call the gospel, is nothing but the good tidings, that the Messiah and his kingdom was come; and so it is to be understood in the New Testament, and so the angel calls it, "good tidings of great joy," Luke ii. 10, bringing the first news of our Saviour's birth. And this seems to be all that his disciples were at that time sent to preach.

So, Luke ix. 59, 60, to him that would have excused his present attendance, because of burying his father; "Jesus said unto him, let the dead bury their dead, but go thou and preach the kingdom of God." When I say, this was all they were to preach, I must be understood that this was the faith they preached; but with it they joined obedience to the Messiah, whom they received for their king. So likewise, when he sent out the seventy, Luke x. their commission was in these words. ver. 9, "Heal the sick, and say unto them, The kingdom of God is come nigh unto you."

After the return of his apostles to him, he sits down with them on a mountain; and a great multitude being gathered about them, St. Luke tells us, chap. ix. 11, "The people followed him, and he received them, and spake unto them of the kingdom of God, and healed them that had need of healing." This was his preaching to this assembly, which consisted of five thousand men, besides women and children: all which great multitude he fed with five loaves and two fishes, Matt. xiv. 21. And what this miracle wrought upon them, St. John tells us, chap. vi. 14, 15, "Then these men, when they had seen the miracle that Jesus did, said, This is of a truth that prophet that should come into the world," i. e. the Messiah. For the Messiah was the only person that they expected from God, and this the time they looked for him. And hence John the Baptist, Matt. xi. 3, styles him, "He that should come;" as in other places, "come from God," or "sent from God," are phrases used for the Messiah.

Here we see our Saviour keep to his usual method of preaching: he speaks to them of the kingdom of God, and does miracles; by which they might understand him to be the Messiah, whose kingdom he spake of. And here we have the reason also, why he so much concealed himself, and forbore to own his being the Messiah. For what the consequence was, of the multitude's but thinking him so, when they were got together, St. John tells us in the very next words: "When Jesus then perceived, that they would come and take him by force to make him a king, he departed again into a mountain himself alone." If they were so ready to set him up for their king, only because they gathered from his miracles that he was the Messiah, whilst he himself said nothing of it: what would not the people have done, and what would not the scribes and pharisees have had an opportunity to accuse him of, if he had openly professed himself to have been the Messiah, that king they looked for? But this we have taken notice of already.

From hence going to Capernaum, whither he was followed by a great part of the people, whom he had the day before so miraculously fed; he, upon the occasion of their following him for the loaves, bids them seek for the meat that endureth to eternal life: and thereupon, John vi. 22—69, declares to them his being sent from the Father; and that those who believed in him, should be raised to eternal life: but all this very much involved in a mixture of allegorical terms of eating, and of bread; bread of life, which came down from heaven, &c. Which is all comprehended and expounded in these short and plain words, ver. 47 and 54, "Verily, verily, I say unto you, he that believeth on me hath everlasting life, and I will raise him up at the last day." The sum of all which discourse is, that he was the Messiah sent from God; and that those who believed him to be so, should be raised from the dead at the last day, to eternal life. These whom he spoke to here were of those who, the day before, would by force have made him king; and therefore it is no wonder he should speak to them of himself, and his kingdom and subjects, in obscure and mystical terms; and such as should offend those who looked for nothing but the grandeur of a temporal kingdom in this world, and the protection and prosperity they had promised themselves under it. The hopes of such a kingdom, now that they had found a man that did miracles, and therefore concluded to be the Deliverer they expected; had the day before almost drawn them into an open insurrection, and involved our Saviour in it. This he thought fit to put a stop to; they still following him, 'tis like, with the same design. And therefore, though he here speaks to them of his kingdom, it was in a way that so plainly baulked their expectation, and shocked them, that when they found themselves disappointed of those vain hopes, and that he talked of their eating his flesh, and drinking his blood, that they might have life; the jews said, ver. 52, "How can this man give us his flesh to eat? And many, even of his disciples said, It was an hard saying: Who can hear it?" And so were scandalized in him, and forsook him, ver. 60, 66. But what the true meaning of this discourse of our Saviour was, the confession of St. Peter, who understood it better, and answered for the rest of the apostles, shows: when Jesus answered him, ver. 67, "Will ye also go away?" Then Simon Peter answered him, "Lord, to whom shall we go? Thou hast the words of eternal life:" i. e. thou teachest us the way to attain eternal life; and accordingly, "we believe, and are sure, that thou art the Messiah, the Son of the living God." This was the eating his flesh and drinking his blood, whereby those who did so had eternal life.

Some time after this, he inquires of his disciples, Mark viii. 27, who the people took him for? They telling him, "for John the Baptist," or one of the old prophets risen from the dead; he asked, What they themselves thought? And here again, Peter answers in these words, Mark viii. 29, "Thou art the Messiah," Luke ix. 20, "The Messiah of God." And Matt. xvi. 16, "Thou art the Messiah, the Son of the living God:" Which expressions, we may hence gather, amount to the same thing. Whereupon our Saviour tells Peter, Matt. xvi. 17, 18, That this was such a truth "as flesh and blood could not reveal to him, but only his Father who was in heaven;" and that this was the foundation, on which he was "to build his church:" by all the parts of which passage it is more than probable, that he had never yet told his apostles in direct words, that he was the Messiah; but that they had gathered it from his life and miracles. For which we may imagine to ourselves this probable reason; because that, if he had familiarly, and in direct terms, talked to his apostles in private, that he was the Messiah the Prince, of whose kingdom he preached so much in public every-where; Judas, whom he knew false and treacherous, would have been readily made use of, to testify against him, in a matter that would have been really criminal to the Roman governor. This, perhaps, may help to clear to us that seemingly abrupt reply of our Saviour to his apostles, John vi. 70, when they confessed him to be the Messiah: I will, for the better explaining of it, set down the passage at large. Peter having said, "We believe and are sure that thou art the Messiah, the Son of the living God; Jesus answered them, Have not I chosen you twelve, and one of you is διά[Editor: illegible character]ολος?" This is a reply, seeming at first sight, nothing to the purpose; when yet it is sure all our Saviour's discourses were wise and pertinent. It seems therefore to me to carry this sense, to be understood afterwards by the eleven (as that of destroying the temple, and raising it again in three days was) when they should reflect on it, after his being betrayed by Judas: you have confessed, and believe the truth concerning me; I am the Messiah your king: but do not wonder at it, that I have never openly declared it to you; for amongst you twelve, whom I have chosen to be with me, there is one who is an informer, or false accuser, (for so the Greek word signifies, and may, possibly, here be so translated, rather than devil) who, if I had owned myself in plain words to have been the "Messiah, the king of Israel," would have betrayed me, and informed against me.

That he was yet cautious of owning himself to his apostles, positively, to be the Messiah, appears farther from the manner wherein he tells Peter, ver. 18, that he will build his church upon that confession of his, that he was the Messiah: I say unto thee, "Thou art Cephas," or a rock, "and upon this rock I will build my church, and the gates of hell shall not prevail against it." Words too doubtful to be laid hold on against him, as a testimony that he professed himself to be the Messiah; especially if we join with them the following words, ver. 19, "And I will give thee the keys of the kingdom of heaven, and what thou shalt bind on earth, shall be bound in heaven; and what thou shalt loose on earth, shall be loosed in heaven." Which being said personally to Peter, render the foregoing words of our Saviour (wherein he declares the fundamental article of his church to be the believing him to be the Messiah) the more obscure and doubtful, and less liable to be made use of against him; but yet such as might afterwards be understood. And for the same reason, he yet, here again, forbids the apostles to say that he was the Messiah, ver. 20.

From this time (say the evangelists) "Jesus began to show to his disciples," i. e. his apostles, (who are often called disciples,) "that he must go to Jerusalem, and suffer many things from the elders, chief priests, and scribes; and be killed, and be raised again the third day," Matt. xvi. 21. These, though all marks of the Messiah, yet how little understood by the apostles, or suited to their expectation of the Messiah, appears from Peter's rebuking him for it in the following words, Matt. xvi. 22. Peter had twice before owned him to be the Messiah, and yet he cannot here bear that he should suffer, and be put to death, and be raised again. Whereby we may perceive, how little yet Jesus had explained to the apostles what personally concerned himself. They had been a good while witnesses of his life and miracles: and thereby being grown into a belief that he was the Messiah, were, in some degree, prepared to receive the particulars that were to fill up that character, and answer the prophecies concerning him. This, from henceforth, he began to open to them (though in a way which the jews could not form an accusation out of;) the time of the accomplishment of all, in his sufferings, death, and resurrection, now drawing on. For this was in the last year of his life: he being to meet the jews at Jerusalem but once more at the passover, and then they should have their will upon him: and, therefore, he might now begin to be a little more open concerning himself: though yet so, as to keep himself out of the reach of any accusation, that might appear just or weighty to the Roman deputy.

After his reprimand to Peter, telling him, "That he savoured not the things of God, but of man," Mark viii. 34, he calls the people to him, and prepares those, who would be his disciples, for suffering, telling them, ver. 38, "Whosoever shall be ashamed of me and my words in this adulterous and sinful generation, of him also shall the Son of man be ashamed, when he cometh in the glory of his Father, with the holy angels:" and then subjoins, Matt. xvi. 27, 28, two great and solemn acts, wherein he would show himself to be the Messiah, the king: "For the Son of man shall come in the glory of his Father, with his angels; and then he shall render to every man according to his works." This is evidently meant of the glorious appearance of his kingdom, when he shall come to judge the world at the last day; described more at large, Matt. xxv. "When the Son of man shall come in his glory, and all the holy angels with him, then shall he sit upon the throne of his glory. Then shall the King say to them on his right hand," &c.

But what follows in the place above quoted, Matt. xvi. 28, "Verily, verily, there be some standing here, who shall not taste of death, till they see the Son of man coming in his kingdom;" importing that dominion, which some there should see him exercise over the nation of the jews; was so covered, by being annexed to the preaching, ver. 27, (where he spoke of the manifestation and glory of his kingdom, at the day of judgment,) that though his plain meaning here in ver. 28, be, that the appearance and visible exercise of his kingly power in his kingdom was so near, that some there should live to see it; yet if the foregoing words had not cast a shadow over these latter, but they had been left plainly to be understood, as they plainly signified; that he should be a King, and that it was so near, that some there should see him in his kingdom; this might have been laid hold on, and made the matter of a plausible and seemingly just accusation against him, by the jews before Pilate. This seems to be the reason of our Saviour's inverting here the order of the two solemn manifestations to the world, of his rule and power; thereby perplexing at present his meaning, and securing himself, as was necessary, from the malice of the jews, which always lay at catch to entrap him, and accuse him to the Roman governor; and would, no doubt, have been ready to have alleged these words, "Some here shall not taste of death, till they see the Son of man coming in his kingdom," against him, as criminal, had not their meaning been, by the former verse, perplexed, and the sense at that time rendered unintelligible, and not applicable by any of his auditors to a sense that might have been prejudicial to him before Pontius Pilate. For how well the chief of the jews were disposed towards him, St. Luke tells us, chap. xi. 54, "Laying wait for him, and seeking to catch something out of his mouth, that they might accuse him;" which may be a reason to satisfy us of the seemingly doubtful and obscure way of speaking, used by our Saviour in other places; his circumstances being such, that without such a prudent carriage and reservedness, he could not have gone through the work which he came to do; nor have performed all the parts of it, in a way correspondent to the descriptions given of the Messiah; and which would be afterwards fully understood to belong to him, when he had left the world.

After this, Matt. xvii. 10, &c. he, without saying it in direct words, begins, as it were, to own himself to his apostles to be the Messiah, by assuring them, that as the scribes, according to the prophecy of Malachi, chap. iv. 5, rightly said, that Elias was to usher in the Messiah; so indeed Elias was already come, though the jews knew him not, and treated him ill; whereby "they understood that he spoke to them of John the Baptist," ver. 13. And a little after he somewhat more plainly intimates, that he is the Messiah, Mark ix. 41, in these words: "Whosoever shall give you a cup of water to drink in my name, because ye belong to the Messiah." This, as I remember, is the first place where our Saviour ever mentioned the name of Messiah; and the first time that he went so far towards the owning, to any of the jewish nation, himself to be him.

In his way to Jerusalem, bidding one follow him, Luke ix. 59, who would first bury his father, ver. 60, "Jesus said unto him, Let the dead bury their dead; but go thou and preach the kingdom of God." And Luke x. 1, sending out the seventy disciples, he says to them, ver. 9, "Heal the sick, and say, The kingdom of God is come nigh unto you." He had nothing else for these, or for his apostles, or any one, it seems, to preach, but the good news of the coming of the kingdom of the Messiah. And if any city would not receive them, he bids them, ver. 10, "Go into the streets of the same, and say, Even the very dust of your city, which cleaveth on us, do we wipe off against you; notwithstanding, be ye sure of this, that the kingdom of God is come nigh unto you." This they were to take notice of, as that which they should dearly answer for, viz. that they had not with faith received the good tidings of the kingdom of the Messiah.

After this, his brethren say unto him, John vii. 2, 3, 4, (the feast of tabernacles being near,) "Depart hence, and go into Judea, that thy disciples also may see the works that thou doest: for there is no man that does any thing in secret, and he himself seeketh to be known openly. If thou do these things, show thyself to the world." Here his brethren, which, the next verse tells us, "did not believe in him," seem to upbraid him with the inconsistency of his carriage; as if he designed to be received for the Messiah, and yet was afraid to show himself: to whom he justified his conduct (mentioned ver. 1.) in the following verses, by telling them, "That the world" (meaning the jews especially) "hated him, because he testified of it, that the works thereof are evil; and that his timew as not yet fully come," wherein to quit his reserve, and abandon himself freely to their malice and fury. Therefore, though he "went up unto the feast," it was "not openly, but, as it were, in secret," ver. 10. And here, coming into the temple about the middle of the feast, he justifies his being sent from God; and that he had not done any thing against the law, in curing the man at the pool of Bethesda, John v. 1—16, on the sabbath-day; which, though done above a year and a half before, they made use of as a pretence to destroy him. But what was the true reason of seeking his life, appears from what we have in this viith chapter, ver. 25—34, "Then said some of them at Jerusalem, Is not this he whom they seek to kill? But lo, he speaketh boldly, and they say nothing unto him. Do the rulers know indeed, that this is the very Messiah? Howbeit, we know this man whence he is; but when the Messiah cometh, no man knoweth whence he is. Then cried Jesus in the temple, as he taught, Ye both know me and ye know whence I am: and I am not come of myself, but he that sent me is true, whom ye know not. But I know him; for I am from him, and he hath sent me. Then they sought [an occasion] to take him, but no man laid hands on him, because his hour was not yet come. And many of the people believed on him, and said, When the Messiah cometh, will he do more miracles than these, which this man hath done? The pharisees heard that the people murmured such things concerning him; and the pharisees and chief priests sent officers to take him. Then said Jesus unto them, Yet a little while am I with you, and then I go to him that sent me: ye shall seek me, and not find me; and where I am, there you cannot come. Then said the jews among themselves, Whither will he go, that we shall not find him?" Here we find that the great fault in our Saviour, and the great provocation to the jews, was his being taken for the Messiah; and doing such things as made the people "believe in him;" i. e. believe that he was the Messiah. Here also our Saviour declares, in words very easy to be understood, at least after his resurrection, that he was the Messiah: for, if he were "sent from God," and did his miracles by the Spirit of God, there could be no doubt but he was the Messiah. But yet this declaration was in a way that the pharisees and priests could not lay hold on, to make an accusation of, to the disturbance of his ministry, or the seizure of his person, how much soever they desired it: for his time was not yet come. The officers they had sent to apprehend him, charmed with his discourse, returned without laying hands on him, ver. 45, 46. And when the chief priests asked them, "Why they brought him not?" They answered, "Never man spake like this man." Whereupon the pharisees reply, "Are ye also deceived? Have any of the rulers, or of the pharisees, believed on him? But this people, who know not the law, are cursed." This shows what was meant "by believing on him," viz. believing that he was the Messiah. For, say they, have any of the rulers, who are skilled in the law, or of the devout and learned pharisees, acknowledged him to be the Messiah? For as for those who in the division among the people concerning him, say, "That he is the Messiah," they are ignorant and vile wretches, know nothing of the scripture, and being accursed, are given up by God, to be deceived by this impostor, and to take him for the Messiah. Therefore, notwithstanding their desire to lay hold on him, he goes on; and ver. 37, 38, "In the last and great day of the feast, Jesus stood and cried, saying, If any man thirst, let him come unto me and drink: he that believeth on me, as the scripture hath said, out of his belly shall flow rivers of living water." And thus he here again declares himself to be the Messiah; but in the prophetic style, as we may see by the next verse of this chapter, and those places in the Old Testament, that these words of our Saviour refer to.

In the next chapter, John viii. all that he says concerning himself, and what they were to believe, tends to this, viz. that he was sent from God his Father; and that, if they did not believe that he was the Messiah, they should die in their sins: but this, in a way, as St. John observes, ver. 27, that they did not well understand. But our Saviour himself tells them, ver. 28, "When ye have lift up the Son of man, then ye shall know that I am he."

Going from them, he cures the man born blind, whom meeting with again, after the jews had questioned him, and cast him out, John ix. 35—38, "Jesus said to him, Dost thou believe on the Son of God? He answered, Who is he, Lord, that I might believe on him? And Jesus said unto him, Thou hast both seen him, and it is he that talketh with thee. And he said, Lord, I believe." Here we see this man is pronounced a believer, when all that was proposed to him to believe, was, that Jesus was "the Son of God," which was, as we have already shown, to believe that he was the Messiah.

In the next chapter, John x. 1—21, he declares the laying down of his life both for jews and gentiles; but in a parable which they understood not, ver. 6—20.

As he was going to the feast of the dedication, the pharisees ask him, Luke xvii. 20, "When the kingdom of God," i. e. of the Messiah, "should come?" He answers, That it should not come with pomp and observation, and great concourse; but that it was already begun amongst them. If he had stopt here, the sense had been so plain, that they could hardly have mistaken him; or have doubted, but that he meant, that the Messiah was already come, and amongst them; and so might have been prone to infer, that Jesus took upon him to be him. But here, as in the place before taken notice of, subjoining to this future revelation of himself, both in his coming to execute vengeance on the jews, and in his coming to judgment, mixed together, he so involved his sense, that it was not easy to understand him. And therefore the jews came to him again in the temple, John x. 23, and said, "How long dost thou make us doubt? If thou be the Christ tell us plainly. Jesus answered, I told you, and ye believed not: the works that I do in my Father's name, they bear witness of me. But ye believed not, because ye are not of my sheep, as I told you." The believing here, which he accuses them of not doing, is plainly their not believing him to be the Messiah, as the foregoing words evince; and in the same sense it is evidently meant in the following verses of this chapter.

From hence Jesus going to Bethabara, and thence returning into Bethany; upon Lazarus's death, John xi. 25—27, Jesus said to Martha, "I am the resurrection and the life; he that believeth in me, though he were dead, yet shall he live; and whosoever liveth and believeth in me shall not die for ever." So I understand ἀποθάνῃ εἰς τὸν αἰῶνα, answerable to ζήσεται εἰς τὸν αἰῶνα, of the septuagint, Gen. iii. 22, or John vi. 51, which we read right, in our English translation, "live for ever." But whether this saying of our Saviour here, can with truth be translated, "He that liveth and believeth in me shall never die," will be apt to be questioned. But to go on, "Believest thou this? She said unto him, Yea, Lord, I believe that thou art the Messiah, the Son of God, which should come into the world." This she gives as a full answer to our Saviour's demands; this being that faith, which, whoever had, wanted no more to make them believers.

We may observe farther, in this same story of the raising of Lazarus, what faith it was our Saviour expected, by what he says, ver. 41, 42, "Father, I thank thee, that thou hast heard me; and I know that thou hearest me always. But because of the people who stand by, I said it, that they may believe that thou hast sent me." And what the consequence of it was, we may see, ver. 45, "Then many of the jews who came to Mary, and had seen the things which Jesus did, believed on him;" which belief was, that he was "sent from the Father;" which, in other words, was, that he was the Messiah. That this is the meaning, in the evangelists, of the phrase, of "believing on him," we have a demonstration in the following words, ver. 47, 48, "Then gathered the chief priests and pharisees a council, and said, What do we? For this man does many miracles; and if we let him alone, all men will believe on him." Those who here say, all men would believe on him, were the chief priests and pharisees, his enemies, who sought his life, and therefore could have no other sense nor thought of this faith in him, which they spake of; but only the believing him to be the Messiah: and that that was their meaning, the adjoining words show: "If we let him alone, all the world will believe on him;" i. e. believe him to be the Messiah. "And the Romans will come and take away both our place and nation." Which reasoning of theirs was thus grounded: If we stand still, and let the people "believe on him," i. e. receive him for the Messiah: they will thereby take him and set him up for their king, and expect deliverance by him; which will draw the Roman arms upon us, to the destruction of us and our country. The Romans could not be thought to be at all concerned in any other belief whatsoever, that the people might have on him. It is therefore plain, that "believing on him," was, by the writers of the gospel, understood to mean the "believing him to be the Messiah." The sanhedrim therefore, ver. 53, 54, from that day forth consulted to put him to death. "Jesus therefore walked not yet" (for so the word ἔτι signifies, and so I think it ought here to be translated) "boldly," or open-faced, "among the jews," i. e. of Jerusalem." Ἔτι cannot well here be translated "no more," because, within a very short time after, he appeared openly at the passover, and by his miracles and speech declared himself more freely than ever he had done; and all the week before his passion, taught daily in the temple, Matt. xx. 17. Mark. x. 32. Luke xviii. 31, &c. The meaning of this place seems therefore to be this: that his time being not yet come, he durst not yet show himself openly and confidently before the scribes and pharisees, and those of the sanhedrim at Jerusalem, who were full of malice against him, and had resolved his death: "But went thence into a country near the wilderness, into a city called Ephraim, and there continued with his disciples," to keep himself out of the way until the passover, "which was nigh at hand," ver. 55. In his return thither, he takes the twelve aside, and tells them before-hand what should happen to him at Jerusalem, whither they were now going; and that all things that are written by the prophets, concerning the Son of man, should be accomplished; that he should be betrayed to the chief priests and scribes: and that they should condemn him to death and deliver him to the gentiles; that he should be mocked, and spit on, and scourged and put to death; and the third day he should rise again. But St. Luke tells us, chap. xviii. 34, That the apostles "understood none of these things, and this saying was hid from them; neither knew they the things which were spoken." They believed him to be the Son of God, the Messiah sent from the Father; but their notion of the Messiah was the same with the rest of the jews, that he should be a temporal prince and deliverer: accordingly we see, Mark x. 35, that, even in this their last journey with him to Jerusalem, two of them, James and John, coming to him, and falling at his feet, said, "Grant unto us that we may sit one on thy right hand, and the other on thy left hand, in thy glory:" or, as St. Matthew has it, chap. xx. 21, "in thy kingdom." That which distinguished them from the unbelieving jews, was, that they believed Jesus to be the very Messiah, and so received him as their King and Lord.

And now, the hour being come that the Son of man should be glorified, he, without his usual reserve, makes his public entry into Jerusalem, riding on a young ass! "As it is written, Fear not, daughter of Sion; behold, thy King cometh, sitting on an ass's colt." But "these things," says St. John, chap. xii. 16, "his disciples understood not, at the first; but when Jesus was glorified, then remembered they that these things were written of him, and that they had done these things unto him." Though the apostles believed him to be the Messiah, yet there were many occurrences of his life, which they understood not (at the time when they happened) to be foretold of the Messiah; which, after his ascension, they found exactly to quadrate. Thus according to what was foretold of him, he rode into the city, "all the people crying, Hosanna, blessed is the King of Israel, that cometh in the name of the Lord." This was so open a declaration of his being the Messiah, that, Luke xix. 39, "Some of the pharisees from among the multitude said unto him, Master, rebuke thy disciples." But he was so far now from stopping them, or disowning this their acknowledgment of his being the Messiah, that he said unto them, "I tell you, that if these should hold their peace, the stones would immediately cry out." And again upon the like occasion of their crying, "Hosanna to the Son of David," in the temple, Matt. xxi. 15, 16, "When the chief priests and scribes were sore displeased, and said unto him, Hearest thou what they say? Jesus said unto them, Yea; have ye never read, Out of the mouths of babes and sucklings thou hast perfected praise?" And now, ver. 14, 15, "He cures the blind and the lame openly in the temple. And when the chief priests and scribes saw the wonderful things that he did, and the children crying in the temple, Hosanna, they were enraged." One would not think, that after the multitude of miracles that our Saviour had now been doing for above three years together, the curing the lame and blind should so much move them. But we must remember, that though his ministry had abounded with miracles, yet the most of them had been done about Galilee, and in parts remote from Jerusalem. There is but one left on record, hitherto done in that city; and that had so ill a reception, that they sought his life for it: as we may read John v. 16. And therefore we hear not of his being at the next passover, because he was there only privately, as an ordinary jew: the reason whereof we may read, John vii. 1, "After these things Jesus walked in Galilee; for he would not walk in Jewry, because the jews sought to kill him."

Hence we may guess the reason why St. John omitted the mention of his being at Jerusalem, at the third passover, after his baptism; probably because he did nothing memorable there. Indeed when he was at the feast of tabernacles, immediately preceding this his last passover, he cured the man born blind: but it appears not to have been done in Jerusalem itself, but in the way, as he retired to the mount of Olives; for there seems to have been nobody by when he did it, but his apostles. Compare ver. 2. with ver. 8, 10, of John ix. This, at least, is remarkable, that neither the cure of this blind man, nor that of the other infirm man, at the passover, above a twelve-month before, at Jerusalem, was done in the sight of the scribes, pharisees, chief priests, or rulers. Nor was it without reason, that in the former part of his ministry, he was cautious of showing himself to them to be the Messiah. But now, that he was come to the last scene of his life, and that the passover was come, the appointed time, wherein he was to complete the work he came for, in his death and resurrection, he does many things in Jerusalem itself before the face of the scribes, pharisees, and whole body of the jewish nation, to manifest himself to be the Messiah. And, as St. Luke says, chap. xix. 47, 48, "he taught daily in the temple: but the chief priests, and the scribes, and the chief of the people, sought to destroy him; and could not find what they might do; for all the people were very attentive to hear him." What he taught we are left to guess, by what we have found him constantly preaching elsewhere: but St. Luke tells us, chap. xx. 1, "He taught in the temple, and evangelized;" or, as we translate it, "preached the gospel;" which, as we have showed, was the making known to them the good news of the kingdom of the Messiah. And this we shall find he did, in what now remains of his history.

In the first discourse of his, which we find upon record, after this, John xii. 20, &c. he foretels his crucifixion, and the belief of all sorts, both jews and gentiles, on him after that. Whereupon the people say to him, ver. 34, "We have heard out of the law, that the Messiah abideth for ever: and how sayest thou, that the Son of man must be lifted up? Who is this Son of man?" In his answer, he plainly designs himself under the name of Light; which was what he had declared himself to them to be, the last time that they had seen him in Jerusalem. For then at the feast of tabernacles, but six months before, he tells them in the very place where he now is, viz. in the temple, "I am the Light of the world; whosoever follows me shall not walk in darkness, but shall have the light of life;" as we may read, John viii. 12. And ix. 5, he says, "As long as I am in the world, I am the Light of the world." But neither here, nor any-where else, does he, even in these four or five last days of his life, (though he knew his hour was come, and was prepared to his death, ver. 27, and scrupled not to manifest himself to the rulers of the jews to be the Messiah, by doing miracles before them in the temple,) ever once in direct words own himself to the jews to be the Messiah; though by miracles and other ways he did every-where make it known unto them, so that it might be understood. This could not be without some reason; and the preservation of his life, which he came now to Jerusalem on purpose to lay down, could not be it. What other could it then be, but the same which had made him use caution in the former part of his ministry; so to conduct himself, that he might do the work which he came for, and in all parts answer the character given of the Messiah, in the law and the prophets? He had fulfilled the time of his ministry; and now taught and did miracles openly in the temple, before the rulers and the people, not fearing to be seized. But he would not be seized for any thing that might make him a criminal to the government: and therefore he avoided giving those, who, in the division that was about him, inclined towards him, occasion of tumult for his sake: or to the jews, his enemies, matter of just accusation, against him, out of his own mouth, by professing himself to be the Messiah, the King of Israel, in direct words. It was enough that by words and deeds he declared it so to them, that they could not but understand him; which it is plain they did, Luke xx. 16, 19. Matt. xxi. 45. But yet neither his actions, which were only doing of good; nor words, which were mystical and parabolical (as we may see, Matt. xxi. and xxii, and the parallel places of Matthew and Luke;) nor any of his ways of making himself known to be the Messiah; could be brought in testimony, or urged against him, as opposite or dangerous to the government. This preserved him from being condemned as a malefactor; and procured him a testimony from the Roman governor, his judge, that he was an innocent man, sacrificed to the envy of the jewish nation. So that he avoided saying that he was the Messiah, that to those who would call to mind his life and death, after his resurrection, he might the more clearly appear to be so. It is farther to be remarked, that though he often appeals to the testimony of his miracles, who he is, yet he never tells the jews, that he was born at Bethlehem, to remove the prejudice that lay against him, whilst he passed for a Galilean, and which was urged as a proof that he was not the Messiah, John vii. 41, 42. The healing of the sick, and doing good miraculously, could be no crime in him, nor accusation against him. But the naming of Bethlehem for his birth-place might have wrought as much upon the mind of Pilate, as it did on Herod's; and have raised a suspicion in Pilate, as prejudicial to our Saviour's innocence as Herod was to the children born there. His pretending to be born at Bethlehem, as it was liable to be explained by the jews could not have failed to have met with a sinister interpretation in the Roman governor, and have rendered Jesus suspected of some criminal design against the government. And hence we see, that when Pilate asked him, John xix. 9, "Whence art thou? Jesus gave him no answer."

Whether our Saviour had not an eye to this straitness, this narrow room that was left to his conduct, between the new converts and the captious jews, when he says, Luke xii. 50, "I have a baptism to be baptized with, and πῶς συνέχομαι, how am I straitened until it be accomplished!" I leave to be considered. "I am come to send fire on the earth," says our Saviour, "and what if it be already kindled?" i. e. There begin already to be divisions about me, John vii. 12, 43, and ix. 16, and x. 19. And I have not the freedom, the latitude, to declare myself openly to be the Messiah; though I am he, that must not be spoken on, until after my death. My way to my throne is closely hedged in on every side, and much straitened; within which I must keep, until it bring me to my cross in its due time and manner; so that it do not cut short the time, nor cross the end of my ministry.

And therefore, to keep up this inoffensive character, and not to let it come within the reach of accident or calumny, he withdrew, with his apostles, out of the town, every evening; and kept himself retired out of the way, Luke xxi. 37. "And in the day-time he was teaching in the temple, and every night he went out and abode in the mount, that is called the Mount of Olives," that he might avoid all concourse to him in the night, and give no occasion of disturbance, or suspicion of himself, in that great conflux of the whole nation of the jews, now assembled in Jerusalem at the passover.

But to return to his preaching in the temple: he bids them, John xii. 36, "To believe in the Light, whilst they have it." And he tells them, ver. 46, "I am the Light come into the world, that every one who believes in me, should not remain in darkness;" which believing in him, was the believing him to be the Messiah, as I have elsewhere showed.

The next day, Matt. xxi. he rebukes them for not having believed John the Baptist, who had testified that he was the Messiah. And then, in a parable, declares himself to be the "Son of God," whom they should destory; and that for it God would take away the kingdom of the Messiah from them, and give it to the gentiles. That they understood him thus, is plain from Luke xxi. 16, "And when they heard it, they said, God forbid." And ver. 19, "For they knew that he had spoken this parable against them."

Much to the same purpose was his next parable, concerning "the kingdom of heaven," Matt. xxi. 1—10. That the jews not accepting of the kingdom of the Messiah, to whom it was first offered, other should be brought in.

The scribes and pharisees and chief priests, not able to bear the declaration he made of himself to be the Messiah (by his discourses and miracles before them, ἔμπροσθεν αὐτῶν, John xii. 37, which he had never done before) impatient of his preaching and miracles, and being not able otherwise to stop the increase of his followers, (for, "said the pharisees among themselves, Perceive ye how ye prevail nothing? Behold, the world is gone after him,") John xii. 19. So that "the chief priests, and the scribes, and the chief of the people sought to destroy him," the first day of his entrance into Jerusalem, Luke xix. 47. The next day again, they were intent upon the same thing, Mark xi. 17, 18, "And he taught in the temple; and the scribes and the chief priests heard it, and sought how they might destroy him; for they feared him, because all the people were astonished at his doctrine."

The next day but one, upon his telling them the kingdom of the Messiah should be taken from them, "The chief priests and scribes sought to lay hands on him the same hour, and they feared the people," Luke xx. 19. If they had so great a desire to lay hold on him, why did they not? They were the chief priests and the rulers, the men of power. The reason St. Luke plainly tells us in the next verse: "And they watched him, and sent forth spies, who should feign themselves just men, that they might take hold of his words, that so they might deliver him unto the power and authority of the governor." They wanted matter of accusation against him, to the power they were under; that they watched for, and that they would have been glad of, if they could have "entangled him in his talk;" as St. Matthew expresses it, chap. xxii. 15. If they could have laid hold on any word, that had dropt from him, that they might have rendered him guilty, or suspected to the Roman governor; that would have served their turn, to have laid hold upon him, with hopes to destroy him. For their power not answering their malice, they could not put him to death by their own authority, without the permission and assistance of the governor; as they confess, John xviii. 31, "It is not lawful for us to put any man to death." This made them so earnest for a declaration in direct words, from his own mouth, that he was the Messiah. It was not that they would more have believed in him, for such a declaration of himself, than they did for his miracles, or other ways of making himself known, which it appears they understood well enough. But they wanted plain direct words, such as might support an accusation, and be of weight before an heathen judge. This was the reason why they pressed him to speak out, John x. 24, "Then came the jews round about him, and said unto him, How long dost thou hold us in suspense? If thou be the Messiah, tell us plainly, παῤῥησία;" i. e. in direct words: for that St. John uses it in that sense we may see, chap. xi. 11—14, "Jesus saith to them, Lazarus sleepeth. His disciples said, If he sleeps, he shall do well. Howbeit, Jesus spake of his death; but they thought he had spoken of taking rest in sleep. Then said Jesus to them plainly, παῤῥησία, Lazarus is dead." Here we see what is meant by παῤῥησία, plain, direct words, such as express the same thing without a figure; and so they would have had Jesus pronounce himself to be the Messiah. And the same thing they press again, Matt. xxvi. 63, the high priest adjuring him by the living God, to tell them whether he were the Messiah the Son of God; as we shall have occasion to take notice by-and-by.

This we may observe in the whole management of their design against his life. It turned upon this, that they wanted and wished for a declaration from him in direct words, that he was the Messiah; something from his own mouth that might offend the Roman power, and render him criminal to Pilate. In the 21st verse of this xxth of Luke, "They asked him, saying, Master, we know that thou sayest and teachest rightly; neither acceptest thou the person of any, but teachest the way of God truly. Is it lawful for us to give tribute to Cæsar, or no?" By this captious question they hoped to catch him, which way soever he answered. For if he had said they ought to pay tribute to Cæsar, it would be plain he allowed their subjection to the Romans; and so in effect disowned himself to be their King and Deliverer; whereby he would have contradicted what his carriage and doctrine seemed to aim at, the opinion that was spread amongst the people, that he was the Messiah. This would have quashed the hopes, and destroyed the faith of those that believed on him; and have turned the ears and hearts of the people from him. If on the other side he answered, No, it is not lawful to pay tribute to Cæsar, they had out of his own mouth wherewithal to condemn him before Pontius Pilate. But St. Luke tells us, ver. 23, "He perceived their craftiness, and said unto them, Why tempt ye me?" i. e. Why do ye lay snares for me? "Ye hypocrites, show me the tribute money;" so it is, Matt. xxii. 19, "Whose image and inscription has it? They said Cæsar's." He said unto them, "Render therefore to Cæsar the things that are Cæsar's, and to God the things that are God's." By the wisdom and caution of which unexpected answer, he defeated their whole design: "and they could not take hold of his words before the people; and they marvelled at his answer, and held their peace." Luke xx. 26. "And leaving him, they departed." Matt. xxii. 22.

He having, by this reply (and what he answered to the sadducees, concerning the resurrection, and to the lawyer about the first commandment, Mark xii.) answered so little to their satisfaction or advantage, they durst ask him no more questions, any of them. And now, their mouths being stopped, he himself begins to question them about the Messiah; asking the pharisees, Matt. xxii. 41, "What think ye of the Messiah? whose son is he? They say unto him, the Son of David." Wherein though they answered right, yet he shows them in the following words, that, however they pretended to be studiers and teachers of the law, yet they understood not clearly the scriptures concerning the Messiah; and thereupon he sharply rebukes their hypocrisy, vanity, pride, malice, covetousness, and ignorance; and particularly tells them, ver. 13, "Ye shut up the kingdom of heaven against men: for ye neither go in yourselves, nor suffer ye them that are entering, to go in." Whereby he plainly declares to them, that the Messiah was come, and his kingdom begun; but that they refused to believe in him themselves, and did all they could to hinder others from believing in him; as is manifest throughout the New Testament; the history whereof sufficiently explains what is meant here by "the kingdom of heaven," which the scribes and pharisees would neither go into themselves, nor suffer others to enter into. And they could not choose but understand him, though he named not himself in the case.

Provoked anew by his rebukes, they get presently to council, Matt. xxvi. 3, 4. "Then assembled together the chief priests, and the scribes and the elders of the people, unto the palace of the high priest, who was called Caiaphas, and consulted that they might take Jesus by subtlety, and kill him. But they said, Not on the feast-day, lest there should be an uproar among the people. For they feared the people," says Luke, chap. xxii. 2.

Having in the night got Jesus into their hands, by the treachery of Judas, they presently led him away bound to Annas, the father-in-law of Caiaphas. Annas, probably, having examined him, and getting nothing out of him for his purpose, sends him away to Caiaphas, John xviii. 24, where the chief priests, the scribes, and the elders were assembled, Matt. xxvi. 57. John xviii. 13, 19. "The high priest then asked Jesus of his disciples, and of his doctrine. Jesus answered him, I spake openly to the world: I ever taught in the synagogue, and in the temple, whither the jews always resort, and in secret have I said nothing." A proof that he had not in private, to his disciples, declared himself in express words to be the Messiah, the Prince. But he goes on: "Why askest thou me?" Ask Judas, who has been always with me. "Ask them who heard me, what I have said unto them; behold, they know what I said." Our Saviour, we see here, warily declines, for the reasons above-mentioned, all discourse of his doctrine. The sanhedrim, Matt. xxvi. 59, "sought false witness against him:" but when "they found none that were sufficient," or came up to the point they desired, which was to have something against him to take away his life (for so I think the words ἴσαι and ἴση mean, Mark xiv. 56, 59.) they try again what they can get out of him himself, concerning his being the Messiah; which, if he owned in express words, they thought they should have enough against him at the tribunal of the Roman governor, to make him "læsæ majestatis reum," and to take away his life. They therefore say to him, Luke xxii. 67, "If thou be the Messiah, tell us." Nay, as St. Matthew hath it, the high priest adjures him by the living God, to tell him whether he were the Messiah. To which our Saviour replies, "If I tell you, ye will not believe; and if I also ask you, ye will not answer me, nor let me go." If I tell you, and prove to you, by the testimony given me from heaven, and by the works that I have done among you, you will not believe in me, that I am the Messiah. Or if I should ask where the Messiah is to be born, and what state he should come in; how he should appear, and other things that you think in me are not reconcileable with the Messiah; you will not answer me, nor let me go, as one that has no pretence to be the Messiah, and you are not afraid should be received for such. But yet I tell you, "Hereafter shall the Son of man sit on the right hand of the power of God," ver. 70. "Then say they all, Art thou then the Son of God? And he said unto them, Ye say that I am." By which discourse with them, related at large here by St. Luke, it is plain, that the answer of our Saviour, set down by St. Matthew, chap. xxvi. 64, in these words, "Thou hast said;" and by St. Mark, chap. xiv. 62, in these, "I am;" is in answer only to this question, "Art thou then the Son of God?" and not to that other, "Art thou the Messiah?" which preceded, and he had answered to before; though Matthew and Mark, contracting the story, set them down together, as if making but one question, omitting all the intervening discourse; whereas it is plain out of St. Luke, that they were two distinct questions, to which Jesus gave two distinct answers. In the first whereof he, according to his usual caution, declined saying in plain express words, that he was the Messiah: though in the latter he owned himself to be "the Son of God." Which though they, being jews, understood to signify the Messiah, yet he knew could be no legal or weighty accusation against him before a heathen; and so it proved. For upon his answering to their question, "Art thou then the Son of God? Ye say that I am;" they cry out, Luke xxii. 71, "What need we any further witness? For we ourselves have heard out of his own mouth." And so thinking they had enough against him, they hurry him away to Pilate. Pilate asking them, John xviii. 29—32, "What accusation bring you against this man? They answered and said, If he were not a malefactor we would not have delivered him up unto thee." Then said Pilate unto them, "Take ye him, and judge him according to your law." But this would not serve their turn, who aimed at his life, and would be satisfied with nothing else. "The jews therefore said unto him, It is not lawful for us to put any man to death." And this was also, "That the saying of Jesus might be fulfilled, which he spake, signifying what death he should die." Pursuing therefore their design of making him appear, to Pontius Pilate, guilty of treason against Cæsar, Luke xxiii. 2, "They began to accuse him, saying, We found this fellow perverting the nation, and forbidding to give tribute to Cæsar; saying, that he himself is the Messiah, the King;" all which were inferences of theirs, from his saying, he was "the Son of God:" which Pontius Pilate finding (for it is consonant that he examined them to the precise words he had said), their accusation had no weight with him. However, the name of king being suggested against Jesus, he thought himself concerned to search it to the bottom, John xviii. 33—37. "Then Pilate entered again into the judgment-hall, and called Jesus, and said unto him, Art thou the king of the jews? Jesus answered him, Sayest thou this of thyself, or did others tell it thee of me? Pilate answered, Am I a jew? Thine own nation and the chief priests have delivered thee unto me: what hast thou done? Jesus answered, My kingdom is not of this world: if my kingdom were of this world, then would my servants fight, that I should not be delivered to the jews; but now my kingdom is not from hence. Pilate therefore said unto him, Art thou a king then? Jesus answered, Thou sayest that I am a king. For this end was I born, and for this cause came I into the world, that I should bear witness to the truth: every one that is of the truth heareth my voice." In this dialogue between our Saviour and Pilate, we may observe, 1. That being asked, Whether he were "The king of the jews?" he answered so, that though he deny it not, yet he avoids giving the least umbrage, that he had any design upon the government. For, though he allows himself to be a king, yet, to obviate any suspicion, he tells Pilate, "his kingdom is not of this world;" and evidences it by this, that if he had pretended to any title to that country, his followers, which were not a few, and were forward enough to believe him their king, would have fought for him, if he had had a mind to set himself up by force, or his kingdom were so to be erected. "But my kingdom," says he, "is not from hence," is not of this fashion, or of this place.

2. Pilate being, by his words and circumstances, satisfied that he laid no claim to his province, or meant any disturbance of the government; was yet a little surprised to hear a man in that poor garb, without retinue, or so much as a servant, or a friend, own himself to be a king; and therefore asks him, with some kind of wonder, "Art thou a king then?"

3. That our Saviour declares, that his great business into the world was, to testify and make good this great truth, that he was a king; i. e. in other words, that he was the Messiah.

4. That whoever were followers of truth, and got into the way of truth and happiness, received this doctrine concerning him, viz. That he was the Messiah, their King.

Pilate being thus satisfied that he neither meant, nor could there arise, any harm from his pretence, whatever it was, to be a king; tells the jews, ver. 31, "I find no fault in this man." But the jews were the more fierce, Luke xxiii. 5. saying, "He stirreth up the people to sedition, by his preaching through all Jewry, beginning from Galilee to this place." And then Pilate, learning that he was of Galilee, Herod's jurisdiction, sent him to Herod; to whom also "the chief priests and scribes," ver. 10, "vehemently accused him." Herod, finding all their accusations either false or frivolous, thought our Saviour a bare object of contempt; and so turning him only into ridicule, sent him back to Pilate: who, calling unto him the chief priests, and the rulers, and the people, ver. 14, "Said unto them, Ye have brought this man unto me, as one that perverteth the people; and behold, I having examined him before you, have found no fault in this man, touching these things whereof ye accuse him; no, nor yet Herod; for I sent you to him: and lo, nothing worthy of death is done by him." And therefore he would have released him: "For he knew the chief priests had delivered him through envy," Mark xv. 10. And when they demanded Barabbas to be released, but as for Jesus, cried, "Crucify him;" Luke xxiii. 22; "Pilate said unto them the third time, Why? What evil hath he done? I have found no cause of death in him; I will, therefore, chastise him, and let him go.

We may observe, in all this whole prosecution of the jews, that they would fain have got it out of Jesus's own mouth, in express words, that he was the Messiah: which not being able to do, with all their heart and endeavour; all the rest that they could allege against him not amounting to a proof before Pilate, that he claimed to be king of the jews; or that he had caused, or done any thing towards a mutiny or insurrection among the people (for upon these two, as we see, their whole charge turned); Pilate again and again pronounced him innocent: for so he did a fourth, and a fifth time; bringing him out to them, after he had whipped him, John xix. 4, 6. And after all, "when Pilate saw that he could prevail nothing, but that rather a tumult was made, he took water, and washed his hands before the multitude, saying, I am innocent of the blood of this just man: see you to it:" Matt. xxvii. 24. Which gives us a clear reason of the cautious and wary conduct of our Saviour, in not declaring himself, in the whole course of his ministry, so much as to his disciples, much less to the multitude, or to the rulers of the jews, in express words, to be the Messiah the King; and why he kept himself always in prophetical or parabolical terms (he and his disciples preaching only the kingdom of God, i. e. of the Messiah, to be come), and left to his miracles to declare who he was; though this was the truth, which he came into the world, as he says himself, John xviii. 37, to testify and which his disciples were to believe.

When Pilate, satisfied of his innocence, would have released him; and the jews persisted to cry out, "Crucify him, crucify him," John xix. 6, "Pilate says to them, Take ye him yourselves, and crucify him: for I do not find any fault in him." The jews then, since they could not make him a state criminal, by alleging his saying, that he was "the Son of God," say, by their law it was a capital crime, ver. 7. "The jews answered to Pilate, We have a law, and by our law he ought to die; because he made himself the Son of God," i. e. because, by saying "he is the Son of God," he has made himself the Messiah, the prophet, which was to come. For we find no other law but that against false prophets, Deut. xviii. 20, whereby "making himself the Son of God," deserved death. After this, Pilate was the more desirous to release him, ver. 12, 13. "But the jews cried out, saying, If thou let this man go, thou art not Cæsar's friend; whosoever maketh himself a king, speaketh against Cæsar." Here we see the stress of their charge against Jesus; whereby they hoped to take away his life, viz. that he "made himself king." We see also upon what they grounded this accusation, viz. because he had owned himself to be "the Son of God." For he had in their hearing, never made or professed himself to be a king. We see here, likewise, the reason why they were so desirous to draw from his own mouth a confession in express words, that he was the Messiah; viz. That they might have what might be a clear proof that he did so. And, last of all, we see reason why, though in expressions which they understood, he owned himself to them to be the Messiah; yet he avoided declaring it to them in such words as might look criminal at Pilate's tribunal. He owned himself to be the Messiah plainly, to the understanding of the jews; but in ways that could not, to the understanding of Pilate, make it appear that he had laid claim to the kingdom of Judea; or went about to make himself king of that country. But whether his saying that he was "the Son of God," was criminal by their law, that Pilate troubled not himself about.

He that considers what Tacitus, Suetonius, Seneca de benef. l. 3. c. 26. say of Tiberius and his reign, will find how necessary it was for our Saviour, if he would not die as a criminal and a traitor, to take great heed to his words and actions; that he did or said not any thing that might be offensive, or give the least umbrage to the Roman government. It behoved an innocent man, who was taken natice of, for something extraordinary in him, to be very wary under a jealous and cruel prince, who encouraged informations, and filled his reign with executions for treason; under whom, words spoken innocently, or in jest, if they could be misconstrued, were made treason, and prosecuted with a rigour, that made it always the same thing to be accused and condemned. And therefore we see, that when the jews told Pilate, John xix. 12, that he should not be a friend to Cæsar, if he let Jesus go (for that whoever made himself king, was a rebel against Cæsar:) he asks them no more whether they would take Barabbas, and spare Jesus, but (though against his conscience) gives him up to death, to secure his own head.

One thing more there is, that gives us light into this wise and necessarily cautious management of himself, which manifestly agrees with it and makes a part of it: and that is, the choice of his apostles: exactly suited to the design and foresight of the necessity of keeping the declaration of the kingdom of the Messiah, which was now expected, within certain general terms, during his ministry. It was not fit to open himself too plainly or forwardly to the heady jews, that he himself was the Messiah; that was to be left to the observation of those who would attend to the purity of his life, the testimony of his miracles, and the conformity of all with the predictions concerning him: by these marks, those he lived amongst were to find it out, without an express promulgation that he was the Messiah until after his death. His kingdom was to be opened to them by degrees, as well to prepare them to receive it, as to enable him to be long enough amongst them, to perform what was the work of the Messiah to be done; and fulfil all those several parts of what was foretold of him in the Old Testament, and we see applied to him in the New.

The jews had no other thoughts of their Messiah, but of a mighty temporal prince, that should raise their nation into an higher degree of power, dominion, and prosperity than ever it had enjoyed. They were filled with the expectation of a glorious earthly kingdom. It was not, therefore, for a poor man, the son of a carpenter, and (as they thought) born in Galilee, to pretend to it. None of the jews, no, not his disciples, could have borne this, if he had expressly avowed this at first, and began his preaching and the opening of his kingdom this way, especially if he had added to it, that in a year or two, he should die an ignominious death upon the cross. They are therefore prepared for the truth by degrees. First, John the Baptist tells them, "The kingdom of God" (a name by which the jews called the kingdom of the Messiah) "is at hand." Then our Saviour comes, and he tells them "of the kingdom of God;" sometimes that it is at hand, and upon some occasions, that it is come; but says, in his public preaching, little or nothing of himself. Then come the apostles and evangelists after his death, and they, in express words, teach what his birth, life, and doctrine had done before, and had prepared the well-disposed to receive, viz. That "Jesus is the Messiah."

To this design and method of publishing the gospel, was the choice of the apostles exactly adjusted; a company of poor, ignorant, illiterate men; who, as Christ himself tells us, Matt. xi. 25, and Luke x. 21, were not of the "wise and prudent" men of the world: they were, in that respect, but mere children. These, convinced by the miracles they saw him daily do, and the unblameable life he led, might be disposed to believe him to be the Messiah: and though they, with others, expected a temporal kingdom on earth, might yet rest satisfied in the truth of their master (who had honoured them with being near his person) that it would come, without being too inquisitive after the time, manner, or seat of his kingdom, as men of letters, more studied in their rabbins, or men of business, more versed in the world, would have been forward to have been. Men, great or wise in knowledge, or ways of the world, would hardly have been kept from prying more narrowly into his design and conduct; or from questioning him about the ways and measures he would take, for ascending the throne; and what means were to be used towards it, and when they should in earnest set about it. Abler men, of higher births or thoughts, would hardly have been hindered from whispering, at least to their friends and relations, that their master was the Messiah; and that, though he concealed himself to a fit opportunity, and until things were ripe for it, yet they should, ere long, see him break out of his obscurity, cast off the cloud, and declare himself, as he was, King of Israel. But the ignorance and lowness of these good, poor men, made them of another temper. They went along, in an implicit trust on him, punctually keeping to his commands, and not exceeding his commission. When he sent them to preach the gospel, he bid them preach "the kingdom of God" to be at hand; and that they did, without being more particular than he had ordered, or mixing their own prudence with his commands, to promote the kingdom of the Messiah. They preached it, without giving, or so much as intimating that their master was he: which men of another condition, and an higher education, would scarce have forborne to have done. When he asked them, who they thought him to be; and Peter answered, "The Messiah, the Son of God," Matt. xvi. 16, he plainly shows by the following words, that he himself had not told them so; and at the same time, ver. 20. forbids them to tell this their opinion of him to any body. How obedient they were to him in this, we may not only conclude from the silence of the evangelists concerning any such thing, published by them any-where before his death; but from the exact obedience three of them paid to a like command of his. He takes Peter, James, and John, into a mountain; and there Moses and Elias coming to him, he is transfigured before them, Matt. xvii. 9. He charges them, saying, "See that ye tell no man what ye have seen, until the Son of man shall be risen from the dead." And St. Luke tells us, what punctual observers they were of his orders in this case, chap. ix. 36, "They kept it close, and told no man in those days, any of those things which they had seen."

Whether twelve other men, of quicker parts, and of a station or breeding, which might have given them any opinion of themselves, or their own abilities, would have been so easily kept from meddling, beyond just what was prescribed them, in a matter they had so much interest in; and have said nothing of what they might, in human prudence, have thought would have contributed to their master's reputation, and made way for his advancement to his kingdom; I leave to be considered. And it may suggest matter of meditation, whether St. Paul was not for this reason, by his learning, parts, and warmer temper, better fitted for an apostle after, than during our Saviour's ministry: and therefore, though a chosen vessel, was not by the divine wisdom called, until after Christ's resurrection.

I offer this only as a subject of magnifying the admirable contrivance of the divine wisdom, in the whole work of our redemption, as far as we are able to trace it, by the footsteps which God hath made visible to human reason. For though it be as easy to omnipotent power to do all things by an immediate over-ruling will, and so to make any instruments work, even contrary to their nature, in subserviency to his ends; yet his wisdom is not usually at the expence of miracles, (if I may so say,) but only in cases that require them, for the evidencing of some revelation or mission to be from him. He does constantly (unless where the confirmation of some truth requires it otherwise) bring about his purposes by means operating according to their natures. If it were not so, the course and evidence of things would be confounded, miracles would lose their name and force; and there could be no distinction between natural and supernatural.

There had been no room left to see and admire the wisdom, as well as innocence of our Saviour, if he had rashly every-where exposed himself to the fury of the jews, and had always been preserved by a miraculous suspension of their malice, or a miraculous rescuing him out of their hands. It was enough for him once to escape from the men of Nazareth, who were going to throw him down a precipice, for him never to preach to them again. Our Saviour had multitudes that followed him for the loaves; who barely seeing the miracles that he did, would have made him king. If to the miracles he did, he had openly added, in express words, that he was the Messiah, and the king they expected to deliver them, he would have had more followers, and warmer in the cause, and readier to set him up at the head of a tumult. These indeed God, by a miraculous influence, might have hindered from any such attempt: but then posterity could not have believed, that the nation of the jews did, at that time, expect the Messiah, their king and deliverer; or that Jesus, who declared himself to be that king and deliverer, showed any miracles amongst them, to convince them of it; or did any thing worthy to make him be credited or received. If he had gone about preaching to the multitude, which he drew after him, that he was the "Messiah, the king of Israel," and this had been evidenced to Pilate; God could indeed, by a supernatural influence upon his mind, have made Pilate pronounce him innocent, and not condemn him as a malefactor, who had openly for three years together, preached sedition to the people, and endeavoured to persuade them, that he was "the Messiah, their king," of the royal blood of David, come to deliver them. But then I ask, Whether posterity would not either have suspected the story, or that some art had been used to gain that testimony from Pilate? Because he could not (for nothing) have been so favourable to Jesus, as to be willing to release so turbulent and seditious a man; to declare him innocent, and to cast the blame and guilt of his death, as unjust, upon the envy of the jews.

But now, the malice of the chief priests, scribes and pharisees; the headiness of the mob, animated with hopes, and raised with miracles; Judas's treachery, and Pilate's care of his government, and of the peace of his province, all working naturally as they should; Jesus, by the admirable wariness of his carriage, and an extraordinary wisdom, visible in his whole conduct; weathers all these difficulties, does the work he comes for, uninterruptedly goes about preaching his full appointed time, sufficiently manifests himself to be the Messiah, in all the particulars the scriptures had foretold of him; and when his hour is come, suffers death: but is acknowledged, both by Judas that betrayed, and Pilate that condemned him, to die innocent. For, to use his own words, Luke xxiv. 46, "Thus it is written, and thus it behoved the Messiah to suffer." And of his whole conduct we have a reason and clear resolution in those words to St. Peter, Matt. xxvi. 53, "Thinkest thou that I cannot now pray to my Father, and he shall presently give me more than twelve legions of angels? But how then shall the scripture be fulfilled, that thus it must be?"

Having this clew to guide us, let us now observe, how our Saviour's preaching and conduct comported with it in the last scene of his life. How cautious he had been in the former part of his ministry, we have already observed. We never find him to use the name of the Messiah but once, until he now came to Jerusalem, this last passover. Before this, his preaching and miracles were less at Jerusalem) where he used to make but very short stays) than any-where else. But now he comes six days before the feast, and is every day in the temple teaching; and there publicly heals the blind and the lame, in the presence of the scribes, pharisees, and chief priests. The time of his ministry drawing to an end, and his hour coming, he cared not how much the chief priests, elders, rulers, and the sanhedrim, were provoked against him by his doctrine and miracles: he was as open and bold in his preaching, and doing the works of the Messiah now at Jerusalem, and in the sight of the rulers, and of all the people; as he had been before cautious and reserved there, and careful to be little taken notice of in that place, and not to come in their way more than needs. All that he now took care of was, not what they should think of him, or design against him, (for he knew they would seize him,) but to say or do nothing that might be a just matter of accusation against him, or render him criminal to the governor. But, as for the grandees of the jewish nation, he spares them not, but sharply now reprehends their miscarriages publicly in the temple; where he calls them more than once, "hypocrites;" as is to be seen, Matt. xxiii. And concludes all with no softer a compellation than "serpents," and "a generation of vipers."

After this severe reproof of the scribes and pharisees, being retired with his disciples into the "Mount of Olives" over against the temple, and there foretelling the destruction of it; his disciples ask him, Matt. xxiv. 3, &c. "When it should be, and what should be the sign of his coming?" He says, to them, "Take heed that no man deceive you: for many shall come in my name," (i. e. taking on them the name and dignity of the Messiah, which is only mine,) saying, "I am the Messiah, and shall deceive many." But be not you by them misled, nor by persecution driven away from this fundamental truth, that I am the Messiah: "for many shall be scandalized," and apostatize; "but he that endures to the end, the same shall be saved: and this gospel of the kingdom shall be preached in all the world:" i. e. the good news of me, the Messiah, and my kingdom, shall be spread through the world. This was the great and only point of belief they were warned to stick to; and this is inculcated again, ver. 23—26, and Mark xiii. 21—23, with this emphatical application to them, in both these evangelists, "Behold, I have told you beforehand; remember, you are forewarned."

This was in answer to the apostles inquiry, concerning his "coming, and the end of the world," ver. 3. For so we translate τῆς συντελείας τ[Editor: illegible character] αἰῶνος. We must understand the disciples here to put their question, according to the notion and way of speaking of the jews. For they had two worlds, as we translate it, ὁ νῦν αἰὼν, καὶ ὁ μέλλων αἰὼν; "the present world," and the "world to come." The kingdom of God, as they called it, or the time of the Messiah, they called ὁ μέλλων αἰὼν, "the world to come," which they believed was to put an end to "this world;" and that then the just should be raised from the dead, to enjoy in that "new world" a happy eternity, with those of the jewish nation, who should be then living.

These two things, viz. the visible and powerful appearance of his kingdom, and the end of the world, being confounded in the apostles question, our Saviour does not separate them, nor distinctly reply to them apart; but, leaving the inquirers in the common opinion, answers at once concerning his coming to take vengeance on the jewish nation, and put an end to their church worship and commonwealth; which was their ὁ νῦν αἰὼν, "present world," which they counted should last till the Messiah came; and so it did, and then had an end put to it. And to this he joins his last coming to judgment, in the glory of his Father, to put a final end to this world, and all the dispensation belonging to the posterity of Adam upon earth. This joining them together, made his answer obscure, and hard to be understood by them then; nor was it safe for him to speak plainer of his kingdom, and the destruction of Jerusalem; unless he had a mind to be accused for having designs against the government. For Judas was amongst them: and whether no other but his apostles were comprehended under the name of "his disciples," who were with him at this time, one cannot determine. Our Saviour, therefore, speaks of his kingdom in no other style, but that which he had all along hitherto used, viz. "the kingdom of God," Luke xxi. 31, "When you see these things come to pass, know ye that the kingdom of God is nigh at hand." And continuing on his discourse with them, he has the same expression, Matt. xxv. 1, "Then the kingdom of heaven shall be like unto ten virgins." At the end of the following parable of the talents, he adds, ver. 31, "When the Son of man shall come in his glory, and all the holy angels with him, then shall he sit upon the throne of his glory. And before him shall be gathered all the nations. And he shall set the sheep on his right hand, and the goats on his left. Then shall the King say," &c. Here he describes to his disciples the appearance of his kingdom, wherein he will show himself a king in glory upon his throne; but this in such a way, and so remote, and so unintelligible to an heathen magistrate; that, if it had been alleged against him, it would have seemed rather the dream of a crazy brain, than the contrivance of an ambitious or dangerous man, designing against the government: the way of expressing what he meant, being in the prophetic style, which is seldom so plain as to be understood, till accomplished. It is plain, that his disciples themselves comprehended not what kingdom he here spoke of, from their question to him after his resurrection, "Wilt thou at this time restore again the kingdom unto Israel?"

Having finished these discourses, he takes order for the passover, and eats it with his disciples; and at supper tells them, that one of them should betray him; and adds, John xiii. 19, "I tell it you now, before it come, that when it is come to pass, you may know that I am." He does not say out, "the Messiah;" Judas should not have that to say against him, if he would; though that be the sense in which he uses this expression, ἐγω εἰμι, "I am," more than once. And that this is the meaning of it, is clear from Mark xii. 6, Luke xxi. 8. In both which evangelists the words are, "For many shall come in my name, saying, ἐγω εἰμι, I am;" the meaning whereof we shall find explained in the parallel place of St. Matthew, chap. xxiv. 5, "For many shall come in my name, saying, ἐγω εἰμι ὁ Χριςὸς, I am the Messiah." Here, in this place of John xiii. Jesus foretels what should happen to him, viz. that he should be betrayed by Judas; adding this prediction to the many other particulars of his death and suffering, which he had at other times foretold to them. And here he tells them the reason of these his predictions, viz. that afterwards they might be a confirmation to their faith. And what was it that he would have them believe, and be confirmed in the belief of? Nothing but this, ὅτι ἐγω εἰμι ὁ Χριςὸς, "that he was the Messiah." The same reason he gives, John xiv. 28, You have heard how I said unto you, I go away, and come again unto you: and now I have told you, before it comes to pass, that when it comes to pass, ye might believe."

When Judas had left them, and was gone out, he talks a little freer to them of his glory and his kingdom, than ever he had done before. For now he speaks plainly of himself, and of his kingdom, John xiii. 31, "Therefore when he [Judas] was gone out, Jesus said, Now is the Son of man glorified, and God is also glorified in him. And, if God be glorified in him, God shall also glorify him in himself, and shall straitway glorify him." And Luke xxii. 29, "And I will appoint unto you a kingdom, as my Father hath appointed unto me; that ye may eat and drink with me at my table, in my kingdom." Though he has every-where, all along through his ministry, preached the "gospel of the kingdom," and nothing else but that and repentance, and the duties of a good life: yet it has been always "the kingdom of God," and "the kingdom of heaven:" and I do not remember, that "any-where, till now, he uses any such expression, as my kingdom." But here now he speaks in the first person, "I will appoint you a kingdom," and, "in my kingdom:" and this we see is only to the eleven, now Judas was gone from them.

With these eleven, whom he was just now leaving, he has a long discourse, to comfort them for the loss of him; and to prepare them for the persecution of the world, and to exhort them to keep his commandments, and to love one another. And here one may expect all the articles of faith should be laid down plainly, if any thing else were required of them to believe, but what he had taught them, and they believed already, viz. "That he was the Messiah." John xiv. 1, "Ye believe in God, believe also in me." Ver. 29, "I have told you before it come to pass, that when it is come to pass, ye may believe." It is believing on him without any thing else. John xvi. 31, "Jesus answered them, Do ye now believe?" This was in answer to their profession, ver. 30, "Now are we sure that thou knowest all things, and needest not that any man should ask thee: by this we believe that thou camest forth from God."

John xvii. 20, "Neither pray I for these alone, but for them also which shall believe on me through their word." All that is spoke of believing, in this his last sermon to them, is only "believing on him," or believing that "he came from God;" which was no other than believing him to be the Messiah.

Indeed, John xiv. 9, our Saviour tells Philip, "He that hath seen me, hath seen the Father." And adds, ver. 10, "Believest thou not that I am in the Father, and the Father in me? The words that I speak unto you, I speak not of myself: but the Father that dwelleth in me, he doth the works." Which being in answer to Philip's words, ver. 9, "Show us the Father," seem to import thus much: "No man hath seen God at any time," he is known only by his works. And that he is my Father, and I the Son of God, i. e. the Messiah, you may know by the works I have done; which it is impossible I could do of myself, but by the union I have with God my Father. For that by being "in God," and "God in him," he signifies such an union with God, that God operates in and by him, appears not only by the words above cited out of ver. 10 (which can scarce otherwise be made coherent sense), but also from the same phrase, used again by our Saviour presently after, ver. 20, "At that day," viz. after his resurrection, when they should see him again, "you shall know that I am in the Father, and you in me, and I in you;" i. e. by the works that I shall enable you to do, through a power I have received from the Father: which whosoever sees me do, must acknowledge the Father to be in me; and whosoever sees you do, must acknowledge me to be in you. And therefore he says, ver. 12, "Verily, verily, I say unto you, he that believeth on me, the works that I do shall he do also, because I go unto my Father." Though I go away, yet I shall be in you, who believe in me; and ye shall be enabled to do miracles also, for the carrying on of my kingdom, as I have done; that it may be manifested to others, that you are sent by me, as I have evidenced to you, that I am sent by the Father. And hence it is that he says, in the immediately preceding ver. 11, "Believe me, that I am in the Father, and the Father in me; if not, believe me for the sake of the works themselves." Let the works that I have done convince you, that I am sent by the Father; that he is with me, and that I do nothing but by his will; and by virtue of the union I have with him; and that consequently I am the Messiah, who am anointed, sanctified, and separated by the Father, to the work for which he sent me.

To confirm them in this faith, and to enable them to do such works as he had done, he promises them the Holy Ghost, John xiv. 25, 26. "These things I have said unto you, being yet present with you." But when I am gone, "The Holy Ghost, the Paraclet," (which may signify Monitor, as well as Comforter, or Advocate,) "which the Father shall send you in my name, he shall show you all things, and bring to your remembrance all things which I have said." So that considering all that I have said, and laying it together, and comparing it with what you shall see come to pass; you may be more abundantly assured, that I am the Messiah; and fully comprehend, that I have done and suffered all things foretold of the Messiah, and that were to be accomplished and fulfilled by him, according to the scriptures. But be not filled with grief, that I leave you, John xvi. 7, "It is expedient for you, that I go away; for if I go not away, the Paraclet will not come unto you." One reason why, if he went not away, the Holy Ghost could not come, we may gather from what has been observed, concerning the prudent and wary carriage of our Saviour all through his ministry, that he might not incur death with the least suspicion of a malefactor. And therefore, though his disciples believed him to be the Messiah, yet they neither understood it so well, nor were so well confirmed in the belief of it, as after that, he being crucified and risen again, they had received the Holy Ghost; and with the gifts of the Holy Spirit, a fuller and clearer evidence and knowledge that he was the Messiah. They then were enlightened to see how his kingdom was such as the scriptures foretold; though not such as they, till then, had expected. And now this knowledge and assurance, received from the Holy Ghost, was of use to them after his resurrection; when they could now boldly go about, and openly preach, as they did, that Jesus was the Messiah; confirming that doctrine by the miracles which the Holy Ghost empowered them to do. But till he was dead and gone, they could not do this. Their going about openly preaching, as they did after his resurrection, that Jesus was the Messiah, and doing miracles every-where, to make it good, would not have consisted with that character of humility, peace and innocence, which the Messiah was to sustain, if they had done it before his crucifixion. For this would have drawn upon him the condemnation of a malefactor, either as a stirrer of sedition against the public peace, or as a pretender to the kingdom of Israel. Hence we see, that they, who before his death preached only the "gospel of the kingdom;" that "the kingdom of God was at hand;" as soon as they had received the Holy Ghost, after his resurrection, changed their style, and everywhere in express words declare, that Jesus is the Messiah, that King which was to come. This, the following words here in St. John xvi. 8—14, confirm; where he goes on to tell them, "And when he is come, he will convince the world of sin; because they believed not on me." Your preaching then, accompanied with miracles, by the assistance of the Holy Ghost, shall be a conviction to the world, that the jews sinned in not believing me to be the Messiah. "Of righteousness," or justice; "because I go to my Father, and ye see me no more." By the same preaching and miracles you shall confirm the doctrine of my ascension; and thereby convince the world, that I was that just one, who am, therefore, ascended to the Father into heaven, where no unjust person shall enter. "Of judgment; because the prince of this world is judged." And by the same assistance of the Holy Ghost ye shall convince the world, that the devil is judged or condemned by your casting of him out, and destroying his kingdom, and his worship, where-ever you preach. Our Saviour adds, "I have yet many things to say unto you, but you cannot bear them now." They were yet so full of a temporal kingdom, that they could not bear the discovery of what kind of kingdom his was, nor what a king he was to be: and therefore he leaves them to the coming of the Holy Ghost, for a farther and fuller discovery of himself, and the kingdom of the Messiah; for fear they should be scandalized in him, and give up the hopes they now had in him, and forsake him. This he tells them, ver. 1, of this xvith chapter: "These things I have said unto you, that you may not be scandalized." The last thing he had told them, before his saying this to them, we find in the last verses of the preceding chapter: "When the Paraclet is come, the Spirit of truth, he shall witness concerning me." He shall show you who I am, and witness it to the world; and then, "Ye also shall bear witness, because ye have been with me from the beginning." He shall call to your mind what I have said and done, that ye may understand it, and know, and bear witness concerning me. And again here, John xvi. after he had told them they could not bear what he had more to say, he adds, ver. 13, "Howbeit, when the Spirit of truth is come, he will guide you into all truth; and he will show you things to come: he shall glorify me." By the Spirit, when he comes, ye shall be fully instructed concerning me; and though you cannot yet, from what I have said to you, clearly comprehend my kingdom and glory, yet he shall make it known to you wherein it consists: and though I am now in a mean state, and ready to be given up to contempt, torment, and death, so that ye know not what to think of it; yet the Spirit, when he comes, "shall glorify me," and fully satisfy you of my power and kingdom; and that I sit on the right hand of God, to order all things for the good and increase of it, till I come again at the last day, in the fulness of glory.

Accordingly, the apostles had a full and clear sight and persuasion of this, after they had received the Holy Ghost; and they preached it every-where boldly and openly, without the least remainder of doubt or uncertainty. But that, even so late as this, they understood not his death and resurrection, is evident from ver. 17, 18, "Then said some of his disciples among themselves, What is it that he saith unto us; A little while, and ye shall not see me; and again, a little while, and ye shall see me; and because I go to the Father? They said therefore, What is this that he saith, A little while? We know not what he saith." Upon which he goes on to discourse to them of his death and resurrection, and of the power they should have of doing miracles. But all this he declares to them in a mystical and involved way of speaking: as he tells them himself, ver. 25, "These things have I spoken to you in proverbs;" i. e. in general, obscure, ænigmatical, or figurative terms (all which, as well as allusive apologues, the jews called proverbs or parables). Hitherto my declaring of myself to you hath been obscure, and with reserve: and I have not spoken of myself to you in plain and direct words, because ye "could not bear it." A Messiah, and not a King, you could not understand: and a King living in poverty and persecution, and dying the death of a slave and malefactor upon a cross; you could not put together. And I had told you in plain words, that I was the Messiah, and given you a direct commission to preach to others, that I professedly owned myself to be the Messiah, you and they would have been ready to have made a commotion, to have set me upon the throne of my father David, and to fight for me; and that your Messiah, your King, in whom are your hopes of a kingdom, should not be delivered up into the hands of his enemies, to be put to death; and of this Peter will instantly give you a proof. But "the time cometh, when I shall no more speak unto you in parables; but I shall show unto you plainly of the Father." My death and resurrection, and the coming of the Holy Ghost, will speedily enlighten you, and then I shall make you know the will and design of my Father; what a kingdom I am to have, and by what means, and to what end, ver. 27. And this the Father himself will show unto you: "For he loveth you, because ye have loved me, and have believed that I came out from the Father." Because ye have believed that I am "the Son of God, the Messiah;" that he hath anointed and sent me; though it hath not yet been fully discovered to you, what kind of kingdom it shall be, nor by what means brought about. And then our Saviour, without being asked, explaining to them what he had said, and making them understand better what before they stuck at, and complained secretly among themselves that they understood not; they thereupon declare, ver. 30, "Now are we sure that thou knowest all things, and needest not that any man should ask thee." It is plain, thou knowest men's thoughts and doubts before they ask. "By this we believe that thou camest forth from God. Jesus answered, Do ye now believe?" Notwithstanding that you now believe, that I came from God, and am the Messiah, sent by him: "Behold, the hour cometh, yea, is now come, that ye shall be scattered;" and as it is Matth. xxvi.

31, and "shall all be scandalized in me." What it is to be scandalized in him, we may see by what followed hereupon, if that which he says to St. Peter, Mark xiv. did not sufficiently explain it.

This I have been the more particular in; that it may be seen, that in this last discourse to his disciples (where he opened himself more than he had hitherto done; and where, if any thing more was required to make them believers than what they already believed, we might have expected they should have heard of it) there were no new articles proposed to them, but what they believed before, viz. that he was the Messiah, the Son of God, sent from the Father; though of his manner of proceeding, and his sudden leaving of the world, and some few particulars, he made them understand something more than they did before. But as to the main design of the gospel, viz. that he had a kingdom, that he should be put to death, and rise again, and ascend into heaven to his Father, and come again in glory to judge the world; this he had told them: and so had acquainted them with the great counsel of God, in sending him the Messiah, and omitted nothing that was necessary to be known or believed in it. And so he tells them himself, John xv. 15, "Henceforth I call you not servants: for the servant knoweth not what his Lord does: but I have called you friends; for all things that I have heard of my Father, I have made known unto you;" though perhaps ye do not so fully comprehend them, as you will shortly, when I am risen and ascended.

To conclude all, in his prayer, which shuts up this discourse, he tells the Father, what he had made known to his apostles; the result whereof we have John xvii. 8, "I have given unto them the words which thou gavest me, and they have received them, and they have believed that thou didst send me." Which is, in effect, that he was the Messiah promised and sent by God. And then he prays for them, and adds, ver. 20, 21, "Neither pray I for these alone, but for them also who shall believe on me through their word." What that word was, through which others should believe in him, we have seen in the preaching of the apostles, all through the history of the Acts, viz. this one great point, that Jesus was the Messiah. The apostles, he says, ver. 25, "know that thou hast sent me;" i. e. are assured that I am the Messiah. And in ver. 21 and 23, he prays, "That the world may believe" (which, ver. 23, is called knowing) "that thou has sent me." So that what Christ would have believed by his disciples, we may see by this his last prayer for them, when he was leaving the world, as by what he preached whilst he was in it.

And, as a testimony of this, one of his last actions, even when he was upon the cross, was to confirm his doctrine, by giving salvation to one of the thieves that was crucified with him, upon his declaration that he believed him to be the Messiah: for so much the words of his request imported, when he said, "Remember me, Lord, when thou comest into thy kingdom," Luke xxiii. 42. To which Jesus replied, ver. 43, "Verily, I say unto thee, To-day shalt thou be with me in paradise." An expression very remarkable: for as Adam, by sin, lost paradise, i. e. a state of happy immortality; here the believing thief, through his faith in Jesus the Messiah, is promised to be put in paradise, and so re-instated in an happy immortality.

Thus our Saviour ended his life. And what he did after his resurrection, St. Luke tells us, Acts i. 3, That he showed himself to the apostles, "forty days, speaking things concerning the kingdom of God." This was what our Saviour preached in the whole course of his ministry, before his passion: and no other mysteries of faith does he now discover to them after his resurrection. All he says, is concerning the kingdom of God; and what it was he said concerning that, we shall see presently out of the other evangelists; having first only taken notice, that when now they asked him, ver. 6, "Lord, wilt thou at this time restore again the kingdom of Israel? He said unto them, ver. 7, It is not for you to know the times and the seasons, which the Father hath put in his own power: but ye shall receive power, after that the Holy Ghost is come upon you; and ye shall be witnesses unto me, unto the utmost parts of the earth." Their great business was to be witnesses to Jesus, of his life, death, resurrection, and ascension; which, put together, were undeniable proofs of his being the Messiah. This was what they were to preach, and what he said to them, concerning the kingdom of God; as will appear by what is recorded of it in the other evangelists.

When on the day of his resurrection he appeared to the two going to Emmaus, Luke xxiv. they declare, ver. 21, what his disciples faith in him was: "But we trusted that it had been he that should have redeemed Israel:" i. e. we believed that he was the Messiah, come to deliver the nation of the jews. Upon this, Jesus tells them they ought to believe him to be the Messiah, notwithstanding what had happened: nay, they ought, by his sufferings and death, to be confirmed in that faith, that he was the Messiah. And ver. 26, 27, "Beginning at Moses and all the prophets, he expounded unto them, in all the scriptures, the things concerning himself," how, "that the Messiah ought to have suffered these things, and to have entered into his glory." Now he applies the prophecies of the Messiah to himself, which we read not, that he did ever do before his passion. And afterwards appearing to the eleven, Luke xxiv. 36, he said unto them, ver. 44—47, "These are the words, which I spake unto you, while I was yet with you, that all things must be fulfilled which are written in the law of Moses, and in the prophets, and in the psalms concerning me. Then opened he their understanding, that they might understand the scripture, and said unto them: Thus it is written, and thus it behoved the Messiah to suffer, and to rise from the dead the third day; and that repentance and remission of sins should be preached in his name among all nations, beginning at Jerusalem." Here we see what it was he had preached to them, though not in so plain open words before his crucifixion; and what it is he now makes them understand; and what it was that was to be preached to all nations, viz. That he was the Messiah that had suffered, and rose from the dead the third day, and fulfilled all things that were written in the Old Testament concerning the Messiah; and that those who believed this, and repented, should receive remission of their sins, through this faith in him. Or, as St. Mark has it, chap. xvi. 15, "Go into all the world, and preach the gospel to every creature; he that believeth, and is baptized, shall be saved; but he that believeth not, shall be damned," ver. 16. What the "gospel," or "good news," was, we have showed already, viz. The happy tidings of the Messiah being come. Ver. 20, And "they went forth and preached every-where, the Lord working with them, and confirming the word with signs following." What the "word" was which they preached, and the Lord confirmed with miracles, we have seen already, out of the history of their Acts. I have already given an account of their preaching every-where, as it is recorded in the Acts, except some few places, where the kingdom of "the Messiah" is mentioned under the name of "the kingdom of God;" which I forbore to set down, till I had made it plain out of the evangelists, that that was no other but the kingdom of the Messiah.

It may be seasonable therefore, now, to add to those sermons we have formerly seen of St. Paul, (wherein he preached no other article of faith, but that Jesus was "the Messiah," the King, who being risen from the dead, now reigneth, and shall more publicly manifest his kingdom, in judging the world at the last day,) what farther is left upon record of his preaching. Acts xix. 8, at Ephesus, "Paul went into the synagogues, and spake boldly for the space of three months;

disputing and persuading, concerning the kingdom of God." And, Acts xx. 25, at Miletus he thus takes leave of the elders of Ephesus: "And now, behold, I know that ye all, among whom I have gone preaching the kingdom of God, shall see my face no more." What this preaching the kingdom of God was, he tells you, ver. 20, 21, "I have kept nothing back from you, which was profitable unto you; but have showed you, and have taught you publickly, and from house to house; testifying both to the jews, and to the Greeks, repentance towards God, and faith towards our Lord Jesus Christ." And so again, Acts xxviii. 23, 24, "When they [the jews at Rome] had appointed him [Paul] a day, there came many to him into his lodging; to whom he expounded and testified the kingdom of God; persuading them concerning Jesus, both out of the law of Moses, and out of the prophets, from morning to evening. And some believed the things which were spoken, and some believed not." And the history of the Acts is concluded with this account of St. Paul's preaching: "And Paul dwelt two whole years in his own hired house, and received all that came in unto him, preaching the kingdom of God, and teaching those things which concern the Lord Jesus the Messiah." We may therefore here apply the same conclusion to the history of our Saviour, writ by the evangelists, and to the history of the apostles, writ in the Acts, which St. John does to his own gospel, chap. xx. 30, 31, "Many other signs did Jesus before his disciples;" and in many other places the apostles preached the same doctrine, "which are not written" in these books; "but these are written that you may believe that Jesus is the Messiah, the Son of God; and that believing you may have life in his name."

What St. John thought necessary and sufficient to be believed, for the attaining eternal life, he here tells us. And this not in the first dawning of the gospel; when, perhaps, some will be apt to think less was required to be believed, than after the doctrine of faith, and mystery of salvation, was more fully explained, in the epistles writ by the apostles, for it is to be remembered, that St. John says this, not as soon as Christ was ascended; for these words, with the rest of St. John's gospel, were not written till many years after not only the other gospels, and St. Luke's history of the Acts, but in all appearance, after all the epistles writ by the other apostles. So that above threescore years after our Saviour's passion (for so long after, both Epiphanius and St. Jerom assure us this gospel was written) St. John knew nothing else required to be believed, for the attaining of life, but that "Jesus is the Messiah, the Son of God."

To this, it is likely, it will be objected by some, that to believe only that Jesus of Nazareth is the Messiah, is but an historical, and not a justifying, or saving faith.

To which I answer, That I allow to the makers of systems and their followers to invent and use what distinctions they please, and to call things by what names they think fit. But I cannot allow to them, or to any man, an authority to make a religion for me, or to alter that which God hath revealed. And if they please to call the believing that which our Saviour and his apostles preached, and proposed alone to be believed, an historical faith; they have their liberty. But they must have a care, how they deny it to be a justifying or saving faith, when our Saviour and his apostles have declared it so to be; and taught no other which men should receive, and whereby they should be made believers unto eternal life: unless they can so far make bold with our Saviour, for the sake of their beloved systems, as to say, that he forgot what he came into the world for; and that he and his apostles did not instruct people right in the way and mysteries of salvation. For that this is the sole doctrine pressed and required to be believed in the whole tenour of our Saviour's and his apostles preaching, we have showed through the whole history of the evangelists and the Acts. And I challenge them to show that there was any other doctrine, upon their assent to which, or disbelief of it, men were pronounced believers or unbelievers; and accordingly received into the church of Christ, as members of his body; as far as mere believing could make them so: or else kept out of it. This was the only gospel-article of faith which was preached to them. And if nothing else was preached every-where, the apostle's argument will hold against any other articles of faith to be believed under the gospel, Rom. x. 14, "How shall they believe that whereof they have not heard?" For to preach any other doctrines necessary to be believed, we do not find that any body was sent.

Perhaps it will farther be urged, that this is not a "saving faith;" because such a faith as this the devils may have, and it was plain they had; for they believed and declared "Jesus to be the Messiah." And St. James, ch. ii. 19, tells us, "The devils believe and tremble;" and yet they shall not be saved. To which I answer, 1. That they could not be saved by any faith, to whom it was not proposed as a means of salvation, nor ever promised to be counted for righteousness. This was an act of grace shown only to mankind. God dealt so favourably with the posterity of Adam, that if they would believe Jesus to be the Messiah, the promised King and Saviour, and perform what other conditions were required of them by the covenant of grace; God would justify them, because of this belief. He would account this faith to them for righteousness, and look on it as making up the defects of their obedience; which being thus supplied, by what was taken instead of it, they were looked on as just or righteous; and so inherited eternal life. But this favour shown to mankind, was never offered to the fallen angels. They had no such proposals made to them: and therefore, whatever of this kind was proposed to men, it availed not devils, whatever they performed of it. This covenant of grace was never offered to them.

2. I answer; that though the devils believed, yet they could not be saved by the covenant of grace; because they performed not the other condition required in it, altogether as necessary to be performed as this of believing: and that is repentance. Repentance is as absolute a condition of the covenant of grace as faith; and as necessary to be performed as that. John the Baptist, who was to prepare the way for the Messiah, "Preached the baptism of repentance for the remission of sins," Mark i. 4.

As John began his preaching with "Repent; for the kingdom of heaven is at hand," Mat. iii. 2; so did our Saviour begin his, Matt. iv. 17, "From that time began Jesus to preach, and to say, Repent; for the kingdom of heaven is at hand." Or, as St. Mark has it in that parallel place, Mark i. 14, 15, "Now, after that John was put in prison, Jesus came into Galilee, preaching the gospel of the kingdom of God, and saying, The time is fulfilled, and the kingdom of God is at hand: repent ye, and believe the gospel." This was not only the beginning of his preaching, but the sum of all that he did preach; viz. That men should repent, and believe the good tidings which he brought them; that "the time was fulfilled" for the coming of the Messiah. And this was what his apostles preached, when he sent them out, Mark vi. 12, "And they, going out, preached that men should repent." Believing Jesus to be the Messiah, and repenting, were so necessary and fundamental parts of the covenant of grace, that one of them alone is often put for both. For here St. Mark mentions nothing but their preaching repentance: as St. Luke, in the parallel place, chap. ix. 6, mentions nothing but their evangelizing, or preaching the good news of the kingdom of the Messiah: and St. Paul often, in his epistles, puts faith for the whole duty of a christian. But yet the tenour of the gospel is what Christ declares, Luke xii. 3, 5, "Unless ye repent, ye shall all likewise perish." And in the parable of the rich man in hell, delivered by our Saviour, Luke xvi. repentance alone is the means proposed, of avoiding that place of torment, ver. 30, 31. And what the tenour of the doctrine which should be preached to the world should be, he tells his apostles, after his resurrection, Luke xxiv. 27, viz. "That repentance and remission of sins" should be preached "in his name," who was the Messiah. And accordingly, believing Jesus to be the Messiah, and repenting, was what the apostles preached. So Peter began, Acts ii. 38, "Repent, and be baptized." These two things were required for the remission of sins, viz. entering themselves in the kingdom of God; and owning and professing themselves the subjects of Jesus, whom they believed to be the Messiah, and received for their Lord and King; for that was to be "baptized in his name:" baptism being an initiating ceremony, known to the jews, whereby those, who leaving heathenism, and professing a submission to the law of Moses, were received into the commonwealth of Israel. And so it was made use of by our Saviour, to be that solemn visible act, whereby those who believed him to be the Messiah, received him as their king, and professed obedience to him, were admitted as subjects into his kingdom: which, in the gospel, is called "the kingdom of God;" and in the Acts and epistles, often by another name, viz. the "Church."

The same St. Peter preaches again to the jews, Acts iii. 19, "Repent, and be converted, that your sins may be blotted out."

What this repentance was which the new covenant required, as one of the conditions to be performed by all those who should receive the benefits of that covenant; is plain in the scripture, to be not only a sorrow for sins past, but (what is a natural consequence of such sorrow, if it be real) a turning from them into a new and contrary life. And so they are joined together, Acts iii. 19, "Repent and turn about;" or, as we render it, "be converted." And Acts xxvi. 20, "Repent and turn to God."

And sometimes "turning about" is put alone to signify repentance, Matt. xiii. 15, Luke xxii. 32, which in other words is well expressed by "newness of life." For it being certain that he, who is really sorry for his sins, and abhors them, will turn from them, and forsake them; either of these acts, which have so natural a connection one with the other, may be, and is often put for both together. Repentance is an hearty sorrow for our past misdeeds, and a sincere resolution and endeavour, to the utmost of our power, to conform all our actions to the law of God. So that repentance does not consist in one single act of sorrow, (though that being the first and leading act gives denomination to the whole,) but in "doing works meet for repentance;" in a sincere obedience to the law of Christ, the remainder of our lives. This was called for by John the Baptist, the preacher of repentance, Matt. iii. 8, "Bring forth fruits meet for repentance." And by St. Paul here, Acts xxvi. 20, "Repent and turn to God, and do works meet for repentance." There are works to follow belonging to repentance, as well as sorrow for what is past.

These two, faith and repentance, i. e. believing Jesus to be the Messiah, and a good life, are the indispensable conditions of the new covenant, to be performed by all those who would obtain eternal life. The reasonableness, or rather necessity of which, that we may the better comprehend, we must a little look back to what was said in the beginning.

Adam being the Son of God, and so St. Luke calls him, chap. iii. 38, had this part also of the likeness and image of his father, viz. that he was immortal. But Adam, transgressing the command given him by his heavenly Father, incurred the penalty; forfeited that state of immortality, and became mortal. After this, Adam begot children: but they were "in his own likeness, after his own image;" mortal, like their father.

God nevertheless, out of his infinite mercy, willing to bestow eternal life on mortal men, sends Jesus Christ into the world; who being conceived in the womb of a virgin (that had not known man) by the immediate power of God, was properly the Son of God; according to what the angel declared unto his mother, Luke i. 30—35, "The Holy Ghost shall come upon thee, and the power of the Highest shall over-shadow thee: therefore also that holy thing, which shall be born of thee, shall be called the Son of God." So that being the Son of God, he was like the Father, immortal; as he tells us, John v. 26, "As the Father hath life in himself, so hath he given to the Son to have life in himself."

And that immortality is a part of that image, wherein those (who were the immediate sons of God, so as to have no other father) were made like their father, appears probable, not only from the places in Genesis concerning Adam, above taken notice of, but seems to me also to be intimated in some expressions, concerning Jesus the Son of God, in the New Testament. Col. i. 15, he is called "the image of the invisible God." Invisible seems put in, to obviate any gross imagination, that he (as images used to do) represented God in any corporeal or visible resemblance. And there is farther subjoined, to lead us into the meaning of it, "The first-born of every creature;" which is farther explained, ver. 18, where he is termed "The first-born from the dead;" thereby making out, and showing himself to be the image of the invisible; that death hath no power over him; but being the Son of God, and not having forfeited that sonship by any transgression; was the heir of eternal life, as Adam should have been, had he continued in his filial duty. In the same sense the apostle seems to use the word image in other places, viz. Rom. viii. 29, "Whom he did foreknow, he also did predestinate to be conformed to the image of his Son, that he might be the first-born among many brethren." This image, to which they were conformed, seems to be immortality and eternal life: for it is remarkable, that in both these places, St. Paul speaks of the resurrection; and that Christ was "The first-born among many brethren;" he being by birth the Son of God, and the others only by adoption, as we see in this same chapter ver. 15—17, "Ye have received the Spirit of adoption, whereby we cry, Abba, Father; the Spirit itself bearing witness with our spirit, that we are the children of God. And if children, then heirs, and joint-heirs with Christ; if so be that we suffer with him, that we may also be glorified together." And hence we see, that our Saviour vouchsafes to call those, who at the day of judgment are, through him, entering into eternal life, his brethren; Matt. xxv. 40, "Inasmuch as ye have done it unto one of the least of these my brethren." May we not in this find a reason, why God so frequently in the New Testament, and so seldom, if at all, in the Old, is mentioned under the single title of the father? And therefore our Saviour says, Matt. xi. "No man knoweth the Father, save the Son, and he to whomsoever the Son will reveal him." God has now a son again in the world, the first-born of many brethren, who all now, by the Spirit of adoption, can say, Abba, Father. And we, by adoption, being for his sake made his brethren, and the sons of God, come to share in that inheritance, which was his natural right; he being by birth the Son of God: which inheritance is eternal life. And again, ver. 23, "We groan within ourselves, waiting for the adoption, to wit, the redemption of our body;" whereby is plainly meant, the change of these frail mortal bodies, into the spiritual immortal bodies at the resurrection; "When this mortal shall have put on immortality," 1 Cor. xv. 54; which in that chapter, ver. 42—44, he farther expresses thus; "So also is the resurrection of the dead. It is sown in corruption, it is raised in incorruption; it is sown in dishonour, it is raised in glory; it is sown in weakness, it is raised in power; it is sown a natural body, it is raised a spiritual body," &c. To which he subjoins, ver. 49, "As we have born the image of the earthly," (i. e. as we have been mortal, like earthy Adam, our father, from whom we are descended, when he was turned out of paradise,) "we shall also bear the image of the heavenly;" into whose sonship and inheritance being adopted, we shall, at the resurrection, receive that adoption we expect, "even the redemption of our bodies;" and after his image, which is the image of the Father, become immortal. Hear what he says himself, Luke xx. 35, 36, "They who shall be accounted worthy to obtain that world, and the resurrection from the dead, neither marry, nor are given in marriage. Neither can they die any more; for they are equal to the angels, and are the sons of god, being the sons of the resurrection." And he that shall read St. Paul's arguing, Acts xiii. 32, 33, will find that the great evidence that Jesus was the "Son of God," was his resurrection. Then the image of his Father appeared in him, when he visibly entered into the state of immortality. For thus the apostle reasons, "We preach to you, how that the promise which was made to our fathers, God hath fulfilled the same unto us, in that he hath raised up Jesus again; as it is also written in the second psalm, Thou art my Son, this day have I begotten thee."

This may serve a little to explain the immortality of the sons of God, who are in this like their Father, made after his image and likeness. But that our Saviour was so, he himself farther declares, John x. 18, where speaking of his life, he says, "No one taketh it from me, but I lay it down of myself; I have power to lay it down, and I have power to take it up again." Which he could not have had, if he had been a mortal man, the son of a man, of the seed of Adam; or else had by any transgression forfeited his life. "For the wages of sin is death;" and he that hath incurred death for his own transgression, cannot lay down his life for another, as our Saviour professes he did. For he was the just one, Acts vii. 52, and xxii. 14, "Who knew no sin;" 2 Cor. v. 21, "Who did no sin, neither was guile found in his mouth." And thus, "As by man came death, so by man came the resurrection of the dead. For as in Adam all die, so in Christ shall all be made alive."

For this laying down his life for others, our Saviour tells us, John x. 17, "Therefore does my Father love me, because I lay down my life, that I might take it again." And this his obedience and suffering was rewarded with a kingdom: which he tells us, Luke xxii. "His Father had appointed unto him:" and which, it is evident out of the epistle to the Hebrews, chap. xii. 2, he had a regard to in his sufferings: "Who for the joy that was set before him, endured the cross, despising the shame, and is set down at the right hand of the throne of God." Which kingdom, given him upon this account of his obedience, suffering, and death, he himself takes notice of in these words, John xvii. 1—4, "Jesus lifted up his eyes to heaven, and said, Father, the hour is come: glorify thy Son, that thy Son also may glorify thee: as thou hast given him power over all flesh, that he should give eternal life to as many as thou hast given him. And this is life eternal, that they may know thee the only true God, and Jesus, the Messiah, whom thou hast sent. I have glorified thee on earth: I have finished the work which thou gavest me to do." And St. Paul, in his epistle to the Philippians, chap. ii. 8—11, "He humbled himself, and became obedient unto death, even the death of the cross. Wherefore God also hath highly exalted him, and given him a name that is above every name; that at the name of Jesus every knee should bow, of things in heaven, and things in earth, and things under the earth; and that every tongue should confess, that Jesus Christ is Lord."

Thus God, we see, designed his Son Jesus Christ a kingdom, an everlasting kingdom in heaven. But though, "as in Adam all die, so in Christ shall all be made alive;" and all men shall return to life again at the last day; yet all men having sinned, and thereby "come short of the glory of God," as St. Paul assures us, Rom. iii. 23, i. e. not attaining to the heavenly kingdom of the Messiah, which is often called the glory of God; (as may be seen, Rom. v. 2, and xv. 7; and ii. 7; Matt. xvi. 27; Mark vii. 38. For no one who is unrighteous, i. e. comes short of perfect righteousness, shall be admitted into the eternal life of that kingdom; as is declared, 1 Cor. vi. 9, "The unrighteous shall not inherit the kingdom of God;") and death, the wages of sin, being the portion of all those who had transgressed the righteous law of God; the son of God would in vain have come into the world to lay the foundations of a kingdom, and gather together a select people out of the world, if, (they being found guilty at their appearance before the judgment-seat of the righteous Judge of all men at the last day,) instead of entrance into eternal life in the kingdom he had prepared for them, they should receive death, the just reward of sin which every one of them was guilty of; this second death would have left him no subjects; and instead of those ten thousand times ten thousand, and thousands of thousands, there would not have been one left him to sing praises unto his name, saying, "Blessing, and honour, and glory, and power, be unto him that sitteth on the throne, and unto the lamb for ever and ever." God therefore, out of his mercy to mankind, and for the erecting of the kingdom of his Son, and furnishing it with subjects out of every kindred, and tongue, and people, and nation; proposed to the children of men, that as many of them as would believe Jesus his Son (whom he sent into the world) to be the Messiah, the promised Deliverer; and would receive him for their King and Ruler; should have all their past sins, disobedience, and rebellion forgiven them: and if for the future they lived in a sincere obedience to his law, to the utmost of their power; the sins of human frailty for the time to come, as well as all those of their past lives; should, for his Son's sake, because they gave themselves up to him, to be his subjects, be forgiven them: and so their faith, which made them be baptized into his name, (i. e. enrol themselves in the kingdom of Jesus the Messiah, and profess themselves his subjects, and consequently live by the laws of his kingdom,) should be accounted to them for righteousness; i. e. should supply the defects of a scanty obedience in the sight of God; who, counting faith to them for righteousness, or complete obedience, did thus justify, or make them just, and thereby capable of eternal life.

Now, that this is the faith for which God of his free grace justifies sinful man, (for "it is God alone that justifieth," Rom. viii. 33, Rom. iii. 26,) we have already showed, by observing through all the history of our Saviour and the apostles, recorded in the evangelists, and in the Acts, what he and his apostles preached, and proposed to be believed. We shall show now, that besides believing him to be the Messiah, their King, it was farther required, that those who would have the privilege, advantage, and deliverance of his kingdom, should enter themselves into it; and by baptism being made denizens, and solemnly incorporated into that kingdom, live as became subjects obedient to the laws of it. For if they believed him to be the Messiah, their King, but would not obey his laws, and would not have him to reign over them; they were but the greater rebels; and God would not justify them for a faith that did but increase their guilt, and oppose diametrically the kingdom and design of the Messiah; "Who gave himself for us, that he might redeem us from all iniquity, and purify unto himself a peculiar people zealous of good works," Titus ii. 14. And therefore St. Paul tells the Galatians, That that which availeth is faith; but "faith working by love." And that faith without works, i. e. the works of sincere obedience to the law and will of Christ, is not sufficient for our justification, St. James shows at large, chap. ii.

Neither, indeed, could it be otherwise; for life, eternal life, being the reward of justice or righteousness only, appointed by the righteous God (who is of purer eyes than to behold iniquity) to those who only had no taint or infection of sin upon them, it is impossible that he should justify those who had no regard to justice at all whatever they believed. This would have been to encourage iniquity, contrary to the purity of his nature; and to have condemned that eternal law of right, which is holy, just, and good; of which no one precept or rule is abrogated or repealed; nor indeed can be, whilst God is an holy, just, and righteous God, and man a rational creature. The duties of that law, arising from the constitution of his very nature, are of eternal obligation; nor can it be taken away or dispensed with, without changing the nature of things, overturning the measures of right and wrong, and thereby introducing and authorizing irregularity, confusion, and disorder in the world. Christ's coming into the world was not for such an end as that; but, on the contrary, to reform the corrupt state of degenerate man; and out of those who would mend their lives, and bring forth fruit meet for repentance, erect a new kingdom.

This is the law of that kingdom, as well as of all mankind; and that law, by which all men shall be judged at the last day. Only those who have believed Jesus to be the Messiah, and have taken him to be their King, with a sincere endeavour after righteousness, in obeying his law; shall have their past sins not imputed to them; and shall have that faith taken instead of obedience, where frailty and weakness made them transgress, and sin prevailed after conversion; in those who hunger and thirst after righteousness, (or perfect obedience,) and do not allow themselves in acts of disobedience and rebellion, against the laws of that kingdom they are entered into.

He did not expect, it is true, a perfect obedience, void of slips and falls: he knew our make, and the weakness of our constitution too well, and was sent with a supply for that defect. Besides, perfect obedience was the righteousness of the law of works; and then the reward would be of debt, and not of grace; and to such there was no need of faith to be imputed to them for righteousness. They stood upon their own legs, were just already, and needed no allowance to be made them for believing Jesus to be the Messiah, taking him for their king, and becoming his subjects. But that Christ does require obedience, sincere obedience, is evident from the law he himself delivers (unless he can be supposed to give and inculcate laws, only to have them disobeyed) and from the sentence he will pass when he comes to judge.

The faith required was, to believe Jesus to be the Messiah, the Anointed: who had been promised by God to the world. Among the jews (to whom the promises and prophecies of the Messiah were more immediately delivered) anointing was used to three sorts of persons, at their inauguration; whereby they were set apart to three great offices, viz. of priests, prophets, and kings. Though these three offices be in holy writ attributed to our Saviour, yet I do not remember that he any-where assumes to himself the title of a priest, or mentions any thing relating to his priesthood; nor does he speak of his being a prophet but very sparingly, and only once or twice, as it were by the by: but the gospel, or the good news of the kingdom of the Messiah, is what he preaches every-where, and makes it his great business to publish to the world. This he did not only as most agreeable to the expectation of the jews, who looked for the Messiah, chiefly as coming in power to be their king and deliverer: but as it best answered the chief end of his coming, which was to be a king, and, as such, to be received by those who would be his subjects in the kingdom which he came to erect. And though he took not directly on himself the title of king, until he was in custody, and in the hands of Pilate; yet it is plain, "King" and "King of Israel," were the familiar and received titles of the Messiah. See John i. 50, Luke xix. 38, compared with Matt. xxi. 9; and Mark xi. 9, John xii. 13, Matt. xxi. 5, Luke xxiii. 2, compared with Matt. xxvii. 11; and John xviii. 33—37, Mark xv. 12, compared with Matt. xxvii. 22, 42.

What those were to do, who believed him to be the Messiah, and received him for their king, that they might be admitted to be partakers with him of his kingdom in glory, we shall best know by the laws he gives them, and requires them to obey; and by the sentence which he himself will give, when sitting on his throne they shall all appear at his tribunal, to receive every one his doom from the mouth of this righteous judge of all men.

What he proposed to his followers to be believed, we have already seen, by examining his and his apostles preaching, step by step, all through the history of the four evangelists, and the Acts of the Apostles. The same method will best and plainest show us, whether he required of those who believed him to be the Messiah, any thing besides that faith, and what it was. For, he being a king, we shall see by his commands what he expects from his subjects: for, if he did not expect obedience to them, his commands would be but mere mockery; and if there were no punishment for the transgressors of them, his laws would not be the laws of a king, and that authority to command, and power to chastise the disobedient, but empty talk, without force, and without influence.

We shall therefore from his injunctions (if any such there be) see what he has made necessary to be performed, by all those who shall be received into eternal life, in his kingdom prepared in the heavens. And in this we cannot be deceived. What we have from his own mouth, especially if repeated over and over again, in different places and expressions, will be past doubt and controversy. I shall pass by all that is said by St. John Baptist, or any other before our Saviour's entry upon his ministry, and public promulgation of the laws of his kingdom.

He began his preaching with a command to repent, as St. Matthew tells us, iv. 17. "From that time Jesus began to preach, saying, Repent; for the kingdom of heaven is at hand." And Luke v. 32, he tells the scribes and pharisees, "I come not to call the righteous;" (those who were truly so, needed no help, they had a right to the tree of life), "but sinners, to repentance."

In his sermon, as it is called, in the mount, Luke vi. and Matt. v. &c. he commands they should be exemplary in good works: "Let your light so shine amongst men, that they may see your good works, and glorify your Father which is in heaven," Matt. v. 15. And that they might know what he came for, and what he expected of them, he tells them, ver. 17—20, "Think not that I am come to dissolve," or loosen, "the law, or the prophets: I am not come to dissolve," or loosen, "but to make it full," or complete; by giving it you in its true and strict sense. Here we see he confirms, and at once re-inforces all the moral precepts in the Old Testament. "For verily I say to you, Till heaven and earth pass, one jot or one tittle, shall in no wise pass from the law, till all be done. Whosoever therefore shall break one of these least commandments, and shall teach men so, he shall be called the least (i, e. as it is interpreted, shall not be at all) in the kingdom of heaven." Ver. 21, "I say unto you, That except your righteousness," i. e. your performance of the eternal law of right, "shall exceed the righteousness of the scribes and pharisees, ye shall in no case enter into the kingdom of heaven." And then he goes on to make good what he said, ver. 17, viz. "That he was come to complete the law," viz. by giving its full and clear sense, free from the corrupt and loosening glosses of the scribes and pharisees, ver. 22—26. He tells them, That not only murder, but causeless anger, and so much as words of contempt, were forbidden. He commands them to be reconciled and kind towards their adversaries; and that upon pain of condemnation. In the following part of his sermon, which is to be read Luke vi. and more at large, Matt. v. vi. vii. he not only forbids actual uncleanness, but all irregular desires, upon pain of hell-fire; causeless divorces; swearing in conversation, as well as forswearing in judgment; revenge; retaliation; ostentation of charity, of devotion, and of fasting; repetitions in prayer, covetousness, worldly care, censoriousness: and on the other side commands loving our enemies, doing good to those that hate us, blessing those that curse us, praying for those that despitefully use us; patience and meekness under injuries, forgiveness, liberality, compassion: and closes all his particular injunctions, with this general golden rule, Matt. vii. 12, "All things whatsoever ye would that men should do to you, do you even so to them, for this is the law and the prophets." And to show how much he is in earnest, and expects obedience to these laws, he tells them, Luke vi. 35, That if they obey, "great shall be their reward;" they "shall be called the sons of the Highest." And to all this, in the conclusion, he adds the solemn sanction; "Why call ye me, Lord, Lord, and do not the things that I say?" It is in vain for you to take me for the Messiah your King, unless you obey me. "Not every one who calls me, Lord, Lord, shall enter into the kingdom of heaven," or be the Sons of God; "but he that doth the will of my father which is in heaven." To such disobedient subjects, though they have prophesied and done miracles in my name, I shall say at the day of judgment, "Depart from me, ye workers of iniquity; I know you not."

When, Matt. xii. he was told, that his mother and brethren sought to speak with him, ver. 49, "Stretching out his hands to his disciples, he said, Behold my mother and my brethren; for whosoever shall do the will of my Father, who is in heaven, he is my brother, and sister, and mother." They could not be children of the adoption, and fellow heirs with him of eternal life, who did not do the will of his heavenly Father.

Matt. xv. and Mark vi. the pharisees finding fault, that his disciples eat with unclean hands, he makes this declaration to his apostles: "Do not ye perceive, that whatsoever from without entereth into a man cannot defile him, because it entereth not into his heart, but his belly? That which cometh out of the man, that defileth the man; for from within, out of the heart of men, proceed evil thoughts, adulteries, fornications, murders, thefts, false witnesses, covetousness, wickedness, deceit, lasciviousness, an evil eye, blasphemy, pride, foolishness. All these ill things come from within, and defile a man."

He commands self-denial, and the exposing ourselves to suffering and danger, rather than to deny or disown him: and this upon pain of losing our souls; which are of more worth than all the world. This we may read, Matt. xvi. 24—27, and the parallel places, Mark viii. and Luke ix.

The apostles disputing among them, who should be greatest in the kingdom of the Messiah, Matt. xviii. 1, he thus determines the controversy, Mark ix. 35, "If any one will be first, let him be last of all, and servant of all:" and setting a child before them adds, Matt. xviii. 3, "Verily I say unto you, Unless ye turn, and become as children, ye shall not enter into the kingdom of heaven."

Matth. xviii. 15, "If thy brother shall trespass against thee, go and tell him his fault between thee and him alone: if he shall hear thee, thou hast gained thy brother. But if he will not hear thee, then take with thee one or two more, that in the mouth of two or three witnesses every word may be established. And if he shall neglect to hear them, tell it to the church: but if he neglect to hear the church, let him be unto thee, as an heathen and publican." Ver. 21, "Peter said, Lord, how often shall my brother sin against me and I forgive him? Till seven times? Jesus said unto him, I say not unto thee, till seven times; but until seventy times seven." And then ends the parable of the servant, who being himself forgiven, was rigorous to his fellow-servant, with these words, ver. 34, "and his Lord was wroth, and delivered him to the tormentors, till he should pay all that was due to him. So likewise shall my heavenly Father do also unto you, if you from your hearts forgive not every one his brother their trespasses."

Luke x. 25, to the lawyer, asking him, "What shall I do to inherit eternal life? He said, What is written in the law? How readest thou?" He answered, "Thou shalt love the Lord thy God with all thy heart, and with all thy soul, and with all thy strength, and with all thy mind; and thy neighbour as thyself." Jesus said, "This do, and thou shalt live." And when the lawyer, upon our Saviour's parable of the good Samaritan, was forced to confess, that he that showed mercy was his neighbour; Jesus dismissed him with this charge, ver. 37, "Go, and do thou likewise."

Luke xi. 41, "Give alms, of such things as ye have; behold all things are clean unto you."

Luke xii. 15, "Take heed, and beware of covetousness." Ver. 22, "Be not solicitous what ye shall eat, or what ye shall drink, nor what ye shall put on;" be not fearful, or apprehensive of want; "for it is your Father's pleasure to give you a kingdom. Sell that you have, and give alms: and provide yourselves bags that wax not old, a treasure in the heavens, that faileth not: for where your treasure is, there will your heart be also. Let your loins be girded, and your lights burning; and ye yourselves like unto men that wait for the Lord when he will return. Blessed are those servants, whom the Lord, when he cometh, shall find watching. Blessed is that servant, whom the Lord having made ruler of his household, to give them their portion of meat in due season, the Lord, when he cometh, shall find so doing. Of a truth I say unto you, that he will make him ruler over all that he hath. But if that servant say in his heart, my Lord delayeth his coming; and shall begin to beat the men servants, and maidens, and to eat and drink, and to be drunken; the Lord of that servant will come in a day when he looketh not for him, and at an hour when he is not aware; and will cut him in sunder, and will appoint him his portion with unbelievers. And that servant who knew his lord's will, and prepared not himself, neither did according to his will, shall be beaten with many stripes. But he that knew not and did commit things worthy of stripes, shall be beaten with few stripes. For unto whomsoever much is given, of him shall much be required: and to whom men have committed much, of him they will ask the more."

Luke xiv. 11, "Whosoever exalteth himself shall be abased: and he that humbleth himself shall be exalted."

Ver. 12, "When thou makest a dinner, or supper, call not thy friends, or thy brethren, neither thy kinsmen, nor thy neighbours; lest they also bid thee again, and a recompense be made thee. But when thou makest a feast, call the poor, and maimed, the lame and the blind; and thou shalt be blessed, for they cannot recompense thee: for thou shalt be recompensed at the resurrection of the just."

Ver. 33, "So likewise, whosoever he be of you, that is not ready to forego all that he hath, he cannot be my disciple."

Luke xiv. 9, "I say unto you, make to yourselves friends of the mammon of unrighteousness: that when ye fail, they may receive you into everlasting habitations. If ye have not been faithful in the unrighteous mammon, who will commit to your trust the true riches? And if ye have not been faithful in that which is another man's, who shall give you that which is your own?"

Luke xvii. 3, "If thy brother trespass against thee, rebuke him; and if he repent forgive him. And if he trespass against thee seven times in a day, and seven times in a day turn again unto thee, saying, I repent, thou shalt forgive him."

Luke xviii. 1. "He spoke a parable to them to this end, that men ought always to pray, and not to faint."

Ver. 18, "One comes to him and asks him, saying, Master, what shall I do to inherit eternal life? Jesus said unto him, If thou wilt enter into life, keep the commandments. He says, Which? Jesus said, Thou knowest the commandments. Thou shalt not kill; thou shalt not commit adultery; thou shalt not steal; thou shalt not bear false witness; defraud not; honour thy father and thy mother; and thou shalt love thy neighbour as thyself. He said, all these have I observed from my youth. Jesus hearing this, loved him, and said unto him, Yet lackest thou one thing: sell all that thou hast, and give it to the poor, and thou shalt have treasure in heaven; and come, follow me." To understand this right, we must take notice, that this young man asks our Saviour, what he must do to be admitted effectually into the kingdom of the Messiah? The jews believed, that when the Messiah came, those of their nation that received him, should not die; but that they, with those who, being dead, should then be raised again by him, should enjoy eternal life with him. Our Saviour, in answer to this demand, tells the young man, that to obtain the eternal life of the kingdom of the Messiah, he must keep the commandments. And then enumerating several of the precepts of the law, the young man says, he had observed these from his childhood. For which the text tells us, Jesus loved him. But our Saviour, to try whether in earnest he believed him to be the Messiah, and resolved to take him to be his king, and to obey him as such, bids him give all that he has to the poor, and come, and follow him; and he should have treasure in heaven. This I look on to be the meaning of the place; this, of selling all he had, and giving it to the poor, not being a standing law of his kingdom; but a probationary command to this young man; to try whether he truly believed him to be the Messiah, and was ready to obey his commands, and relinquish all to follow him, when he, his prince, required it.

And therefore we see, Luke xix. 14, where our Saviour takes notice of the jews not receiving him as the Messiah, he expresses it thus: "We will not have this man to reign over us." It is not enough to believe him to be the Messiah, unless we also obey his laws, and take him to be our king to reign over us.

Matt. xxii. 11—13, he that had not on the wedding-garment, though he accepted of the invitation, and came to the wedding, was cast into utter darkness. By the wedding-garment, it is evident good works are meant here; that wedding-garment of fine linen, clean, and white, which we are told, Rev. xix, 8, is the δικαιώματα, "righteous acts of the saints;" or, as St. Paul calls it, Ephes. iv. 1, "The walking worthy of the vocation wherewith we are called." This appears from the parable itself: "The kingdom of heaven," says our Saviour, ver. 2, "is like unto a king, who made a marriage for his son." And here he distinguishes those who were invited, into three sorts: 1. Those who were invited, and came not; i. e. those who had the gospel, the good news of the kingdom of God proposed to them, but believed not. 2. Those who came, but had not on a wedding-garment; i. e. believed Jesus to be the Messiah, but were not new clad (as I may so say) with a true repentance, and amendment of life: nor adorned with those virtues, which the apostle, Col. iii. requires to be put on. 3. Those who were invited, did come, and had on the wedding-garment; i. e. heard the gospel, believed Jesus to be the Messiah, and sincerely obeyed his laws. These three sorts are plainly designed here; whereof the last only were the blessed, who were to enjoy the kingdom prepared for them.

Matt. xxiii. "Be not ye called Rabbi; for one is your master, even the Messiah, and ye are all brethren. And call no man your father upon the earth: for one is your Father which is in heaven. Neither be ye called masters: for one is your master, even the Messiah. But he that is greatest amongst you, shall be your servant. And whosoever shall exalt himself, shall be abased; and he that shall humble himself, shall be exalted."

Luke xxi. 34, "Take heed to yourselves, lest your hearts be at any time overcharged with surfeiting and drunkenness, and cares of this life."

Luke xxii. 25, "He said unto them, the kings of the gentiles exercise lordship over them; and they that exercise authority upon them, are called benefactors. But ye shall not be so. But he that is greatest among you, let him be as the younger; and he that is chief, as he that doth serve."

John xiii. 34, "A new commandment I give unto you, That ye love one another: as I have loved you, that ye also love one another. By this shall all men know that ye are my disciples, if ye love one another." This command, of loving one another, is repeated again, chap. xv. 12, and 17.

John xiv. 15, "If ye love me, keep my commandments." Ver. 21, "He that hath my commandments, and keepeth them, he it is that loveth me: and he that loveth me, shall be loved of my Father, and I will love him, and manifest myself to him." Ver. 23, "If a man loveth me he will keep my words." Ver. 24, "He that loveth me not, keepeth not my sayings."

John xv. 8, "In this is my Father glorified, that ye bear much fruit; so shall ye be my disciples." Ver. 14, "Ye are my friends, if ye do whatsoever I command you."

Thus we see our Saviour not only confirmed the moral law; and clearing it from the corrupt glosses of the scribes and pharisees, showed the strictness as well as obligation of its injunctions;

but moreover, upon occasion, requires the obedience of his disciples to several of the commands he afresh lays upon them; with the inforcement of unspeakable rewards and punishments in another world, according to their obedience or disobedience. There is not, I think, any of the duties of morality, which he has not, somewhere or other, by himself and his apostles, inculcated over and over again to his followers in express terms. And is it for nothing that he is so instant with them to bring forth fruit? Does he, their King, command, and is it an indifferent thing? Or will their happiness or misery not at all depend upon it, whether they obey or no? They were required to believe him to be the Messiah; which faith is of grace promised to be reckoned to them, for the completing of their righteousness, wherein it was defective: but righteousness, or obedience to the law of God, was their great business, which, if they could have attained by their own performances, there would have been no need of this gracious allowance, in reward of their faith: but eternal life, after the resurrection, had been their due by a former covenant, even that of works; the rule whereof was never abolished, though the rigour was abated. The duties enjoined in it were duties still. Their obligations had never ceased; nor a wilful neglect of them was ever dispensed with. But their past transgressions were pardoned, to those who received Jesus, the promised Messiah, for their king; and their future slips covered, if renouncing their former iniquities, they entered into his kingdom, and continued his subjects with a steady resolution and endeavour to obey his laws. This righteousness therefore, a complete obedience, and freedom from sin, are still sincerely to be endeavoured after. And it is no-where promised, that those who persist in a wilful disobedience to his laws, shall be received into the eternal bliss of his kingdom, how much soever they believe in him.

A sincere obedience, how can any one doubt to be, or scruple to call, a condition of the new covenant, as well as faith; whoever reads our Saviour's sermon in the mount, to omit all the rest? Can any thing be more express than these words of our Lord? Matt. vi. 14, "If you forgive men their trespasses, your heavenly Father will also forgive you: but if you forgive not men their trespasses, neither will your Father forgive your trespasses." And John xiii. 17, "If ye know these things, happy are ye if you do them." This is so inindispensable a condition of the new covenant, that believing without it, will not do, nor be accepted; if our Saviour knew the terms on which he would admit men into life. "Why call ye me, Lord, Lord," says he, Luke vi. 46, "and do not the things which I say?" It is not enough to believe him to be the Messiah, the Lord, without obeying him. For that these he speaks to here, were believers, is evident from the parallel place, Matt. vii. 21—23, where it is thus recorded: "Not every one who says, Lord, Lord, shall enter into the kingdom of heaven; but he that doth the will of my father, which is in heaven." No rebels, or refractory disobedient, shall be admitted there, though they have so far believed in Jesus, as to be able to do miracles in his name: as is plain out of the following words: "Many will say to me in that day, Have we not prophesied in thy name, and in thy name have cast out devils, and in thy name have done many wonderful works? And then will I profess unto them, I never knew you; depart from me, ye workers of iniquity."

This part of the new covenant, the apostles also, in their preaching the gospel of the Messiah, ordinarily joined with the doctrine of faith.

St. Peter, in his first sermon, Acts ii. when they were pricked in heart, and asked, "What shall we do?" says, ver. 38, "Repent, and be baptized, every one of you in the name of Jesus Christ, for the remission of sins." The same he says to them again in his next speech, Acts iv. 26, "Unto you first, God having raised up his Son Jesus, sent him to bless you." How was this done? "in turning away every one from your iniquities."

The same doctrine they preach to the high priest and rulers, Acts v. 30, "The God of our fathers raised up Jesus, whom ye slew, and hanged on a tree. Him hath God exalted with his right hand, to be a Prince and a Saviour, for to give repentance to Israel, and forgiveness of sins; and we are witnesses of these things, and so is also the Holy Ghost, whom God hath given to them that obey him."

Acts xvii. 30, St. Paul tells the Athenians, That now under the gospel, "God commandeth all men everywhere to repent."

Acts xx. 21, St. Paul, in his last conference with the elders of Ephesus, professes to have taught them the whole doctrine necessary to salvation: "I have," says he, "kept back nothing that was profitable unto you; but have showed you, and have taught you publicly, and from house to house; testifying both to the jews and to the Greeks:" and then gives an account what his preaching had been, viz. "Repentance towards God, and faith towards our Lord Jesus the Messiah." This was the sum and substance of the gospel which St. Paul preached, and was all that he knew necessary to salvation; viz. "Repentance, and believing Jesus to be the Messiah:" and so takes his last farewell of them, whom he shall never see again, ver. 32, in these words, "And now, brethren, I commend you to God, and to the word of his grace, which is able to build you up, and to give you an inheritance among all them that are sanctified." There is an inheritance conveyed by the word and covenant of grace: but it is only to those who are sanctified.

Acts xxiv. 24, "When Felix sent for Paul," that he and his wife Drusilla might hear him, "concerning the faith in Christ;" Paul reasoned of righteousness, or justice; and temperance; the duties we owe to others, and to ourselves; and of the judgment to come; until he made Felix to tremble. Whereby it appears, that "temperance and justice" were fundamental parts of the religion that Paul professed, and were contained in the faith which he preached. And if we find the duties of the moral law not pressed by him every-where, we must remember, that most of his sermons left upon record, were preached in their synagogues to the jews, who acknowledged their obedience due to all the precepts of the law; and would have taken it amiss to have been suspected not to have been more zealous for the law than he. And therefore it was with reason that his discourses were directed chiefly to what they yet wanted, and were averse to, the knowledge and embracing of Jesus, their promised Messiah. But what his preaching generally was, if we will believe him himself, we may see, Acts xxvi. where giving an account to king Agrippa, of his life and doctrine, he tells him, ver. 20, "I showed unto them of Damascus, and at Jerusalem, and throughout all the coasts of Judea, and then to the gentiles, that they should repent and turn to God, and do works meet for repentance."

Thus we see, by the preaching of our Saviour and his apostles, that he required of those who believed him to be the Messiah, and received him for their Lord and Deliverer, that they should live by his laws: and that (though in consideration of their becoming his subjects, by faith in him, whereby they believed and took him to be the Messiah, their former sins should be forgiven, yet) he would own none to be his, nor receive them as true denizens of the new Jerusalem, into the inheritance of eternal life; but leave them to the condemnation of the unrighteous; who renounced not their former miscarriages, and lived in a sincere obedience to his commands. What he expects from his followers, he has sufficiently declared as a legislator: and that they may not be deceived, by mistaking the doctrine of faith, grace, free-grace, and the pardon and forgiveness of sins, and salvation by him, (which was the great end of his coming,) he more than once declares to them, for what omissions and miscarriages he shall judge and condemn to death, even those who have owned him, and done miracles in his name: when he comes at last to render to every one according to what he had done in the flesh, sitting upon his great and glorious tribunal, at the end of the world.

The first place where we find our Saviour to have mentioned the day of judgment, is John v. 28, 29, in these words: "the hour is coming, in which all that are in their grave shall hear his [i. e. the Son of God's] voice, and shall come forth; they that have done good, unto the resurrection of life; and they that have done evil, unto the resurrection of damnation." That which puts the distinction, if we will believe our Saviour, is the having done good or evil. And he gives a reason of the necessity of his judging or condemning those "who have done evil," in the following words, ver. 30, "I can of myself do nothing. As I hear I judge; and my judgment is just; because I seek not my own will, but the will of my Father who hath sent me." He could not judge of himself; he had but a delegated power of judging from the Father, whose will he obeyed in it; and who was of purer eyes than to admit any unjust person into the kingdom of heaven.

Matt. vii. 22, 23, speaking again of that day, he tells what his sentence will be, "Depart from me, ye workers of iniquity." Faith in the penitent and sincerely obedient, supplies the defect of their performances; and so by grace they are made just. But we may observe, none are sentenced or punished for unbelief, but only for their misdeeds. "They are workers of iniquity" on whom the sentence is pronounced.

Matt. xiii. 41, "At the end of the world, the Son of man shall send forth his angels; and they shall gather out of his kingdom all scandals, and them which do iniquity; and cast them into a furnace of fire; there shall be wailing and gnashing of teeth." And again, ver. 49, "The angels shall sever the wicked from among the just; and shall cast them into the furnace of fire."

Matt. xvi. 24, "For the Son of man shall come in the glory of his Father, with his angels: and then he shall reward every man according to his works."

Luke xiii. 26, "Then shall ye begin to say, We have eaten and drank in thy presence, and thou hast taught in our streets. But he shall say, I tell you, I know you not; depart from me, ye workers of iniquity."

Matt. xxv. 31—46, "When the Son of man shall come in his glory; and before him shall be gathered all nations; he shall set the sheep on his right hand, and the goats on his left. Then shall the king say to them on his right hand, Come, ye blessed of my Father, inherit the kingdom prepared for you from the foundation of the world; for I was an hungered, and ye gave me meat; I was thirsty, and ye gave me drink; I was a stranger, and ye took me in; naked, and ye clothed me; I was sick, and ye visited me; I was in prison, and ye came unto me. Then shall the righteous answer him, saying, Lord, when saw we thee an hungered, and fed thee? &c. And the King shall answer and say unto them, Verily, I say unto you, Inasmuch as ye have done it unto one of the least of these my brethren, ye have done it unto me. Then shall he say unto them on the left hand, Depart from me, ye cursed, into everlasting fire, prepared for the devil and his angels: for I was an hungered, and ye gave me no meat; I was thirsty, and ye gave me no drink; I was a stranger, and ye took me not in; naked, and ye clothed me not; sick, and in prison, and ye visited me not. Insomuch that ye did it not to one of these, ye did it not to me. And these shall go into everlasting punishment; but the righteous into life eternal."

These, I think, are all the places where our Saviour mentions the last judgment, or describes his way of proceeding in that great day; wherein, as we have observed, it is remarkable, that every-where the sentence follows doing or not doing, without any mention of believing or not believing. Not that any, to whom the gospel hath been preached, shall be saved, without believing Jesus to be the Messiah: for all being sinners, and transgressors of the law, and so unjust; are all liable to condemnation; unless they believe, and so through grace are justified by God, for this faith, which shall be accounted to them for righteousness. But the rest wanting this cover, this allowance for their transgressions, must answer for all their actions; and being found transgressors of the law, shall, by the letter and sanction of that law, be condemned for not having paid a full obedience to that law; and not for want of faith. That is not the guilt on which the punishment is laid; though it be the want of faith, which lays open their guilt uncovered; and exposes them to the sentence of the law, against all that are unrighteous.

The common objection here, is, If all sinners shall be condemned, but such as have a gracious allowance made them; and so are justified by God, for believing Jesus to be the Messiah, and so taking him for their King, whom they are resolved to obey to the utmost of their power; "What shall become of all mankind, who lived before our Saviour's time, who never heard of his name, and consequently could not believe in him?" To this the answer is so obvious and natural, that one would wonder how any reasonable man should think it worth the urging. No-body was, or can be required to believe, what was never proposed to him to believe. Before the fulness of time, which God from the counsel of his own wisdom had appointed to send his Son in, he had, at several times, and in different manners, promised to the people of Israel, an extraordinary person to come; who, raised from amongst themselves, should be their Ruler and Deliverer. The time, and other circumstances of his birth, life, and person, he had in sundry prophecies so particularly described, and so plainly foretold, that he was well known, and expected by the jews, under the name of the Messiah, or Anointed, given him in some of these prophecies. All then that was required, before his appearing in the world, was to believe what God had revealed, and to rely with a full assurance on God, for the performance of his promise; and to believe, that in due time he would send them the Messiah, this anointed King, this promised Saviour and Deliverer, according to his word. This faith in the promises of God, this relying and acquiescing in his word and faithfulness, the Almighty takes well at our hands, as a great mark of homage, paid by us poor frail creatures, to his goodness and truth, as well as to his power and wisdom: and accepts it as an acknowledgment of his peculiar providence, and benignity to us. And therefore our Saviour tells us, John xii. 44, "He that believes on me, believes not on me, but on him that sent me." The works of nature show his wisdom and power; but it is his peculiar care of mankind most eminently discovered in his promises to them, that shows his bounty and goodness; and consequently engages their hearts in love and affection to him. This oblation of an heart, fixed with dependence on, and affection to him, is the most acceptable tribute we can pay him, the foundation of true devotion, and life of all religion. What a value he puts on this depending on his word, and resting satisfied in his promises, we have an example in Abraham; whose faith "was counted to him for righteousness," as we have before remarked out of Rom. iv. And his relying firmly on the promise of God, without any doubt of its performance, gave him the name of the father of the faithful; and gained him so much favour with the Almighty, that he was called the "friend of God;" the highest and most glorious title that can be bestowed on a creature. The thing promised was no more but a son by his wife Sarah; and a numerous posterity by him, which should possess the land of Canaan. These were but temporal blessings, and (except the birth of a son) very remote, such as he should never live to see, nor in his own person have the benefit of. But because he questioned not the performance of it; but rested fully satisfied in the goodness, truth, and faithfulness of God, who had promised, it was counted to him for righteousness. Let us see how St. Paul expresses it, Rom. iv. 18—22, "Who, against hope, believed in hope, that he might become the father of many nations; according to that which was spoken, So shall thy seed be. And being not weak in faith, he considered not his own body now dead, when he was above an hundred years old, neither yet the deadness of Sarah's womb. He staggered not at the promise of God through unbelief, but was strong in faith: giving glory to God, and being fully persuaded, that what he had promised he was able to perform. And therefore it was imputed to him for righteousness." St. Paul having here emphatically described the strength and firmness of Abraham's faith, informs us, that he thereby "gave glory to God;" and therefore it was accounted to him for righteousness." This is the way that God deals with poor frail mortals. He is graciously pleased to take it well of them, and give it the place of righteousness, and a kind of merit in his sight; if they believe his promises, and have a steadfast relying on his veracity and goodness. St. Paul, Heb. xi. 6, tells us, "Without faith it is impossible to please God:" but at the same time tells us what faith that is. "For," says he, "he that cometh to God, must believe that he is; and that he is a rewarder of them that diligently seek him." He must be persuaded of God's mercy and goodwill to those who seek to obey him; and rest assured of his rewarding those who rely on him, for whatever, either by the light of nature, or particular promises, he has revealed to them of his tender mercies, and taught them to expect from his bounty. This description of faith (that we might not mistake what he means by that faith, without which we cannot please God, and which recommended the saints of old) St. Paul places in the middle of the list of those who were eminent for their faith; and whom he sets as patterns to the converted Hebrews, under persecution, to encourage them to persist in their confidence of deliverance by the coming of Jesus Christ, and in their belief of the promises they now had under the gospel. By those examples he exhorts them not to "draw back" from the hope that was set before them, nor apostatize from the profession of the christian religion. This is plain from ver. 35—38, of the precedent chapter: "Cast not away therefore your confidence, which hath great recompence of reward. For ye have great need of persisting or perseverance;" (for so the Greek word signifies here, which our translation renders "patience." Vide Luke viii. 15.) "that after ye have done the will of God, ye might receive the promise. For yet a little while, and he that shall come will come, and will not tarry. Now the just shall live by faith. But if any man draw back, my soul shall have no pleasure in him."

The examples of faith, which St. Paul enumerates and proposes in the following words, chap. xi. plainly show, that the faith whereby those believers of old pleased God, was nothing but a steadfast reliance on the goodness and faithfulness of God, for those good things, which either the light of nature, or particular promises, had given them grounds to hope for. Of what avail this faith was with God, we may see, ver. 4, "By faith Abel offered unto God a more excellent sacrifice than Cain; by which he obtained witness that he was righteous." Ver. 5, "By faith Enoch was translated, that he should not see death: for before his translation he had this testimony, that he pleased God." Ver. 7, "Noah being warned of God of things not seen as yet;" being wary, "by faith prepared an ark, to the saving of his house; by the which he condemned the world, and became heir of the righteousness which is by faith." And what it was that God so graciously accepted and rewarded, we are told, ver. 11, "Through faith also Sarah herself received strength to conceive seed, and was delivered of a child, when she was past age." How she came to obtain this grace from God, the apostle tells us, "Because she judged him faithful who had promised." Those therefore, who pleased God, and were accepted by him before the coming of Christ, did it only by believing the promises, and relying on the goodness of God, as far as he had revealed it to them. For the apostle, in the following words, tells us, ver. 13, "These all died in faith, not having received (the accomplishment of) the promises; but having seen them afar off: and were persuaded of them, and embraced them." This was all that was required of them; to be persuaded of, and embrace the promises which they had. They could be "persuaded of" no more than was proposed to them; "embrace" no more than was revealed; according to the promises they had received, and the dispensations they were under. And if the faith of things "seen afar off;" if their trusting in God for the promises he then gave them; if a belief of the Messiah to come; were sufficient to render those who lived in the ages before Christ acceptable to God, and righteous before him: I desire those who tell us, that God will not (nay, some go so far as to say, cannot) accept any, who do not believe every article of their particular creeds and systems, to consider, why God, out of his infinite mercy, cannot as well justify men now, for believing Jesus of Nazareth to be the promised Messiah, the King and Deliverer; as those heretofore, who believed only that God would, according to his promise, in due time, send the Messiah, to be a King and Deliverer.

There is another difficulty often to be met with, which seems to have something of more weight in it: and that is, that "though the faith of those before Christ (believing that God would send the Messiah, to be a Prince and a Saviour to his people, as he had promised), and the faith of those since his time (believing Jesus to be that Messiah, promised and sent by God), shall be accounted to them for righteousness; yet what shall become of all the rest of mankind, who, having never heard of the promise or news of a Saviour; not a word of a Messiah to be sent, or that was come; have had no thought or belief concerning him?"

To this I answer; that God will require of every man, "according to what a man hath, and not according to what he hath not." He will not expect the improvement of ten talents, where he gave but one; nor require any one should believe a promise of which he has never heard. The apostle's reasoning, Rom. x. 14, is very just: "How shall they believe in him, of whom they have not heard?" But though there be many who being strangers to the commonwealth of Israel, were also strangers to the oracles of God, committed to that people; many, to whom the promise of the Messiah never came, and so were never in a capacity to believe or reject that revelation; yet God had, by the light of reason, revealed to all mankind, who would make use of that light, that he was good and merciful. The same spark of the divine nature and knowledge in man, which making him a man, showed him the law he was under, as a man; showed him also the way of atoning the merciful, kind, compassionate Author and Father of him and his being, when he had transgressed that law. He that made use of this candle of the Lord, so far as to find what was his duty, could not miss to find also the way to reconciliation and foregiveness, when he had failed of his duty: though, if he used not his reason this way, if he put out or neglected this light, he might, perhaps, see neither.

The law is the eternal, immutable standard of right. And a part of that law is, that a man should forgive, not only his children, but his enemies, upon their repentance, asking pardon, and amendment. And therefore he could not doubt that the author of this law, and God of patience and consolation, who is rich in mercy, would forgive his frail offspring, if they acknowledged their faults, disapproved the iniquity of their transgressions, begged his pardon, and resolved in earnest, for the future, to conform their actions to this rule, which they owned to be just and right. This way of reconciliation, this hope of atonement, the light of nature revealed to them: and the revelation of the gospel, having said nothing to the contrary, leaves them to stand and fall to their own Father and Master, whose goodness and mercy is over all his works.

I know some are forward to urge that place of the Acts, chap. iv. as contrary to this. The words, ver. 10 and 12, stand thus: "Be it known unto you all, and to all the people of Israel, that by the name of Jesus Christ of Nazareth, whom ye crucified, whom God raised from the dead, even by him, doth this man" [i. e. the lame man restored by Peter] "stand here before you whole. This is the stone which is set at nought by you builders, which is become the head of the corner. Neither is there salvation in any other: for there is none other name under heaven given among men, in which we must be saved." Which, in short, is, that Jesus is the only true Messiah, neither is there any other person, but he, given to be a mediator between God and man; in whose name we may ask, and hope for salvation.

It will here possibly be asked, "Quorsum perditio hæc?" What need was there of a Saviour? What advantage have we by Jesus Christ?

It is enough to justify the fitness of any thing to be done, by resolving it into the "wisdom of God," who had done it; though our short views, and narrow understandings, may utterly incapacitate us to see that wisdom, and to judge rightly of it. We know little of this visible, and nothing at all of the state of that intellectual world, wherein are infinite numbers and degrees of spirits out of the reach of our ken, or guess; and therefore know not what transactions there were between God and our Saviour, in reference to his kingdom. We know not what need there was to set up an head and a chieftain, in opposition to "the prince of this world, the prince of the power of the air," &c. whereof there are more than obscure intimations in scripture. And we shall take too much upon us, if we shall call God's wisdom or providence to account, and pertly condemn for needless all that our weak, and perhaps biassed, understanding cannot account for.

Though this general answer be reply enough to the forementioned demand, and such as a rational man, or fair searcher after truth, will acquiesce in; yet in this particular case, the wisdom and goodness of God has shown itself so visibly to common apprehensions, that it hath furnished us abundantly wherewithal to satisfy the curious and inquisitive; who will not take a blessing, unless they be instructed what need they had of it, and why it was bestowed upon them. The great and many advantages we receive by the coming of Jesus the Messiah, will show, that it was not without need, that he was sent into the world.

The evidence of our Saviour's mission from heaven is so great, in the multitude of miracles he did before all sorts of people, that what he delivered cannot but be received as the oracles of God, and unquestionable verity. For the miracles he did were so ordered by the divine providence and wisdom, that they never were, nor could be denied by any of the enemies, or opposers of christianity.

Though the works of nature, in every part of them, sufficiently evidence a deity; yet the world made so little use of their reason, that they saw him not, where, even by the impressions of himself, he was easy to be found. Sense and lust blinded their minds in some, and a careless inadvertency in others, and fearful apprehensions in most, (who either believed there were, or could not but suspect there might be, superiour unknown beings,) gave them up into the hands of their priests, to fill their heads with false notions of the Deity, and their worship with foolish rites, as they pleased: and what dread or craft once began, devotion soon made sacred, and religion immutable. In this state of darkness and ignorance of the true God, vice and superstition held the world. Nor could any help be had, or hoped for, from reason; which could not be heard, and was judged to have nothing to do in the case; the priests, everywhere, to secure their empire, having excluded reason from having any thing to do in religion. And in the crowd of wrong notions, and invented rites, the world had almost lost the sight of the one only true God. The rational and thinking part of mankind, it is true, when they sought after him, they found the one supreme, invisible God; but if they acknowledged and worshipped him, it was only in their own minds. They kept this truth locked up in their own breasts as a secret, nor ever durst venture it amongst the people; much less amongst the priests, those wary guardians, of their own creeds and profitable inventions. Hence we see, that reason, speaking ever so clearly to the wise and virtuous, had never authority enough to prevail on the multitude; and to persuade the societies of men, that there was but one God, that alone was to be owned and worshipped. The belief and worship of one God, was the national religion of the Israelites alone: and if we will consider it, it was introduced and supported amongst the people by revelation. They were in Goshen, and had light, whilst the rest of the word were in almost Egyptian darkness, "without God in the world." There was no part of mankind, who had quicker parts, or improved them more; that had a greater light of reason, or followed it farther in all sorts of speculations, than the Athenians; and yet we find but one Socrates amongst them, that opposed and laughed at their polytheism, and wrong opinions of the Deity; and we see how they rewarded him for it. Whatsoever Plato, and the soberest of the philosophers, thought of the nature and being of the one God, they were fain, in their outward professions and worship, to go with the herd, and keep to their religion established by law: which what it was, and how it had disposed the minds of these knowing and quick-sighted Grecians, St. Paul tells us, Acts xvii. 22—29, "Ye men of Athens," says he, "I perceive, that in all things ye are too superstitious. For as I passed by, and beheld your devotions, I found an altar with this inscription, to the unknown god. Whom therefore ye ignorantly worship, him declare I unto you. God that made the world, and all things therein, seeing that he is Lord of heaven and earth, dwelleth not in temples made with hands: neither is worshipped with men's hands, as though he needed any thing, seeing that he giveth unto all life, and breath, and all things; and hath made of one blood all the nations of men, for to dwell on the face of the earth; and hath determined the times before appointed, and the bounds of their habitations; that they should seek the Lord, if haply they might feel him out and find him, though he be not far from every one of us." Here he tells the Athenians, that they, and the rest of the world (given up to superstition) whatever light there was in the works of creation and providence, to lead them to the true God; yet few of them found him. He was every-where near them; yet they were but like people groping and feeling for something in the dark, and did not see him with a full and clear day-light; "but thought the Godhead like to gold and siver, and stone, graven by art and man's device."

In this state of darkness and errour, in reference to the "true God," our Saviour found the world. But the clear revelation he brought with him, dissipated this darkness; made the "one invisible true God" known to the world: and that with such evidence and energy, that polytheism and idolatry have no-where been able to withstand it: but wherever the preaching of the truth he delivered, and the light of the gospel hath come, those mists have been dispelled. And, in effect, we see, that since our Saviour's time, the "belief of one God" has prevailed and spread itself over the face of the earth. For even to the light that the Messiah brought into the world with him, we must ascribe the owning and profession of one God, which the mahometan religion hath derived and borrowed from it. So that in this sense it is certainly and manifestly true of our Saviour, what St. John says of him, 1 John iii. 8, "For this purpose the Son of God was manifested, that he might destroy the works of the devil." This light the world needed, and this light is received from him: that there is but "one God," and he "eternal, invisible;" not like to any visible objects, nor to be represented by them.

If it be asked, whether the revelation to the patriarchs by Moses did not teach this, and why that was not enough? The answer is obvious; that however clearly the knowledge of one invisible God, maker of heaven and earth, was revealed to them; yet that revelation was shut up in a little corner of the world; amongst a people, by that very law, which they received with it, excluded from a commerce and communication with the rest of mankind. The gentile world, in our Saviour's time, and several ages before, could have no attestation of the miracles on which the Hebrews built their faith, but from the jews themselves, a people not known to the greatest part of mankind; contemned and thought vilely of, by those nations that did know them; and therefore very unfit and unable to propagate the doctrine of one God in the world, and diffuse it through the nations of the earth, by the strength and force of that ancient revelation, upon which they had received it. But our Saviour, when he came, threw down this wall of partition; and did not confine his miracles or message to the land of Canaan, or the worshippers at Jerusalem. But he himself preached at Samaria, and did miracles in the borders of Tyre and Sidon, and before multitudes of people gathered from all quarters. And after his resurrection, sent his apostles amongst the nations, accompanied with miracles; which were done in all parts so frequently, and before so many witnesses of all sorts, in broad day-light, that, as I have before observed, the enemies of christianity have never dared to deny them; no, not Julian himself: who neither wanted skill nor power to inquire into the truth: nor would have failed to have proclaimed and exposed it, if he could have detected any falsehood in the history of the gospel; or found the least ground to question the matter of fact published of Christ and his apostles. The number and evidence of the miracles done by our Saviour and his followers, by the power and force of truth, bore down this mighty and accomplished emperor, and all his parts, in his own dominions. He durst not deny so plain a matter of fact, which being granted, the truth of our Saviour's doctrine and mission unavoidably follows; notwithstanding whatsoever artful suggestions his wit could invent, or malice should offer to the contrary.

Next to the knowledge of one God; maker of all things; "a clear knowledge of their duty was wanting to mankind." This part of knowledge, though cultivated with some care by some of the heathen philosophers, yet got little footing among the people. All men, indeed, under pain of displeasing the gods, were to frequent the temples: every one went to their sacrifices and services: but the priests made it not their business to teach them virtue. If they were diligent in their observations and ceremonies; punctual in their feasts and solemnities, and the tricks of religion; the holy tribe assured them the gods were pleased, and they looked no farther. Few went to the schools of the philosophers to be instructed in their duties, and to know what was good and evil in their actions. The priests sold the better pennyworths, and therefore had all the custom. Lustrations and processions were much easier than a clean conscience, and a steady course of virtue; and an expiatory sacrifice that atoned for the want of it, was much more convenient than a strict and holy life. No wonder then, that religion was everywhere distinguished from, and preferred to virtue; and that it was dangerous heresy and profaneness to think the contrary. So much virtue as was necessary to hold societies together, and to contribute to the quiet of governments, the civil laws of commonwealths taught, and forced upon men that lived under magistrates. But these laws being for the most part made by such, who had no other aims but their own power, reached no farther than those things that would serve to tie men together in subjection; or at most were directly to conduce to the prosperity and temporal happiness of any people. But natural religion, in its full extent, was no-where, that I know, taken care of, by the force of natural reason. It should seem, by the little that has hitherto been done in it, that it is too hard a task for unassisted reason to establish morality in all its parts, upon its true foundation, with a clear and convincing light. And it is at least a surer and shorter way, to the apprehensions of the vulgar, and mass of mankind, that one manifestly sent from God, and coming with visible authority from him, should, as a king and law-maker, tell them their duties; and require their obedience; than leave it to the long and sometimes intricate deductions of reason, to be made out to them. Such trains of reasoning the greatest part of mankind have neither leisure to weigh; nor, for want of education and use, skill to judge of. We see how unsuccessful in this the attempts of philosophers were before our Saviour's time. How short their several systems came of the perfection of a true and complete morality, is very visible. And if, since that, the christian philosophers have much out-done them: yet we may observe, that the first knowledge of the truths they have added, is owing to revelation: though as soon as they are heard and considered, they are found to be agreeable to reason; and such as can by no means be contradicted. Every one may observe a great many truths, which he receives at first from others, and readily assents to, as consonant to reason, which he would have found it hard, and perhaps beyond his strength, to have discovered himself. Native and original truth is not so easily wrought out of the mine, as we, who have it delivered already dug and fashioned into our hands, are apt to imagine. And how often at fifty or threescore years old are thinking men told what they wonder how they could miss thinking of? Which yet their own contemplations did not, and possibly never would have helped them to. Experience shows, that the knowledge of morality, by mere natural light, (how agreeable soever it be to it,) makes but a slow progress, and little advance in the world. And the reason of it is not hard to be found in men's necessities, passions, vices, and mistaken interests; which turn their thoughts another way: and the designing leaders, as well as following herd, find it not to their purpose to employ much of their meditations this way. Or whatever else was the cause, it is plain, in fact, that human reason unassisted failed men in its great and proper business of morality. It never from unquestionable principles, by clear deductions, made out an entire body of the "law of nature." And he that shall collect all the moral rules of the philosophers, and compare them with those contained in the New Testament, will find them to come short of the morality delivered by our Saviour, and taught by his apostles; a college made up, for the most part, of ignorant, but inspired fishermen.

Though yet, if any one should think, that out of the sayings of the wise heathens before our Saviour's time, there might be a collection made of all those rules of morality, which are to be found in the christian religion; yet this would not at all hinder, but that the world, nevertheless, stood as much in need of our Saviour, and the morality delivered by him. Let it be granted (though not true) that all the moral precepts of the gospel were known by somebody or other, amongst mankind before. But where, or how, or of what use, is not considered. Suppose they may be picked up here and there; some from Solon and Bias in Greece, others from Tully in Italy: and to complete the work, let Confucius, as far as China, be consulted; and Anacharsis, the Scythian, contribute his share. What will all this do, to give the world a complete morality, that may be to mankind the unquestionable rule of life and manners? I will not here urge the impossibility of collecting from men, so far distant from one another, in time and place, and languages. I will suppose there was a Stobeus in those times, who had gathered the moral sayings from all the sages of the world. What would this amount to, towards being a steady rule; a certain transcript of a law that we are under? Did the saying of Aristippus, or Confucius, give it an authority? Was Zeno a law-giver to mankind? If not, what he or any other philosopher delivered, was but a saying of his. Mankind might hearken to it, or reject it, as they pleased; or as it suited their interest, passions, principles or humours. They were under no obligation; the opinion of this or that philosopher was of no authority. And if it were, you must take all he said under the same character. All his dictates must go for law, certain and true; or none of them. And then, if you will take any of the moral sayings of Epicurus (many whereof Seneca quotes with esteem and approbation) for precepts of the law of nature, you must take all the rest of his doctrine for such too; or else his authority ceases: and so no more is to be received from him, or any of the sages of old, for parts of the law of nature, as carrying with it an obligation to be obeyed, but what they prove to be so. But such a body of ethics, proved to be the law of nature, from principles of reason, and teaching all the duties of life; I think nobody will say the world had before our Saviour's time. It is not enough, that there were up and down scattered sayings of wise men, conformable to right reason. The law of nature, is the law of convenience too: and it is no wonder that those men of parts, and studious of virtue, (who had occasion to think on any particular part of it,) should, by meditation, light on the right even from the observable convenience and beauty of it; without making out its obligation from the true principles of the law of nature, and foundations of morality. But these incoherent apophthegms of philosophers, and wise men, however excellent in themselves, and well intended by them; could never make a morality, whereof the world could be convinced; could never rise to the force of a law, that mankind could with certainty depend on. Whatsoever should thus be universally useful, as a standard to which men should conform their manners, must have its authority, either from reason or revelation. It is not every writer of morality, or compiler of it from others, that can thereby be erected into a law-giver to mankind; and a dictator of rules, which are therefore valid, because they are to be found in his books; under the authority of this or that philosopher. He, that any one will pretend to set up in this kind, and have his rules pass for authentic directions, must show, that either he builds his doctrine upon principles of reason, self-evident in themselves; and that he deduces all the parts of it from thence, by clear and evident demonstration: or must show his commission from heaven, that he comes with authority from God, to deliver his will and commands to the world. In the former way, no-body that I know, before our Saviour's time, ever did, or went about to give us a morality. It is true, there is a law of nature: but who is there that ever did, or undertook to give it us all entire, as a law; no more, nor no less, than what was contained in, and had the obligation of that law? Who ever made out all the parts of it, put them together, and showed the world their obligation? Where was there any such code, that mankind might have recourse to, as their unerring rule, before our Saviour's time? If there was not, it is plain there was need of one to give us such a morality; such a law, which might be the sure guide of those who had a desire to go right; and, if they had a mind, need not mistake their duty, but might be certain when they had performed, when failed in it. Such a law of morality Jesus Christ hath given us in the New Testament; but by the latter of these ways, by revelation. We have from him a full and sufficient rule for our direction, and conformable to that of reason. But the truth and obligation of its precepts have their force, and are put past doubt to us, by the evidence of his mission. He was sent by God: his miracles show it; and the authority of God in his precepts cannot be questioned. Here morality has a sure standard, that revelation vouches, and reason cannot gainsay, nor question; but both together witness to come from God the great law-maker. And such an one as this, out of the New Testament, I think the world never had, nor can any one say, is any-where else to be found. Let me ask any one, who is forward to think that the doctrine of morality was full and clear in the world, at our Saviour's birth; whither would he have directed Brutus and Cassius, (both men of parts and virtue, the one whereof believed, and the other disbelieved a future being,) to be satisfied in the rules and obligations of all the parts of their duties; if they should have asked him, Where they might find the law they were to live by, and by which they should be charged, or acquitted, as guilty, or innocent? If to the sayings of the wise, and the declarations of philosophers, he sends them into a wild wood of uncertainty, to an endless maze, from which they should never get out: if to the religions of the world, yet worse: and if to their own reason, he refers them to that which had some light and certainty; but yet had hitherto failed all mankind in a perfect rule; and we see, resolved not the doubts that had arisen amongst the studious and thinking philosophers; nor had yet been able to convince the civilized parts of the world, that they had not given, nor could, without a crime, take away the lives of their children, by exposing them.

If any one shall think to excuse human nature, by laying blame on men's negligence, that they did not carry morality to an higher pitch; and make it out entire in every part, with that clearness of demonstration which some think it capable of; he helps not the matter. Be the cause what it will, our Saviour found mankind under a corruption of manners and principles, which ages after ages had prevailed, and must be confessed, was not in a way or tendency to be mended. The rules of morality were in different countries and sects different. And natural reason no-where had cured, nor was like to cure the defects and errours in them. Those just measures of right and wrong, which necessity had anywhere introduced, the civil laws prescribed, or philosophy recommended, stood on their true foundations. They were looked on as bonds of society, and conveniencies of common life, and laudable practices. But where was it that their obligation was thoroughly known and allowed, and they received as precepts of a law; of the highest law, the law of nature? That could not be, without a clear knowledge and acknowledgment of the law-maker, and the great rewards and punishments, for those that would, or would not obey him. But the religion of the heathens, as was before observed, little concerned itself in their morals. The priests, that delivered the oracles of heaven, and pretended to speak from the gods, spoke little of virtue and a good life. And, on the other side, the philosophers, who spoke from reason, made not much mention of the Deity in their ethics. They depended on reason and her oracles, which contain nothing but truth: but yet some parts of that truth lie too deep for our natural powers easily to reach, and make plain and visible to mankind; without some light from above to direct them. When truths are once known to us, though by tradition, we are apt to be favourable to our own parts; and ascribe to our own understandings the discovery of what, in reality, we borrowed from others: or, at least, finding we can prove, what at first we learn from others, we are forward to conclude it an obvious truth, which, if we had sought, we could not have missed. Nothing seems hard to our understandings that is once known: and because what we see, we see with our own eyes; we are apt to overlook, or forget the help we had from others who showed it us, and first made us see it; as if we were not at all beholden to them, for those truths they opened the way to, and led us into. For knowledge being only of truths that are perceived to be so, we are favourable enough to our own faculties, to conclude, that they of their own strength would have attained those discoveries, without any foreign assistance; and that we know those truths, by the strength and native light of our own minds, as they did from whom we received them by theirs, only they had the luck to be before us. Thus the whole stock of human knowledge is claimed by every one, as his private possession, as soon as he (profiting by others discoveries) has got it into his own mind: and so it is; but not properly by his own single industry, nor of his own acquisition. He studies, it is true, and takes pains to make a progress in what others have delivered: but their pains were of another sort, who first brought those truths to light, which he afterwards derives from them. He that travels the roads now, applauds his own strength and legs that have carried him so far in such a scantling of time; and ascribes all to his own vigour; little considering how much he owes to their pains, who cleared the woods, drained the bogs, built the bridges, and made the ways passable; without which he might have toiled much with little progress. A great many things which we have been bred up in the belief of, from our cradles, (and are notions grown familiar, and, as it were, natural to us, under the gospel,) we take for unquestionable obvious truths, and easily demonstrable; without considering how long we might have been in doubt or ignorance of them, had revelation been silent. And many are beholden to revelation, who do not acknowledge it. It is no diminishing to revelation, that reason gives its suffrage too, to the truths revelation has discovered. But it is our mistake to think, that because reason confirms them to us, we had the first certain knowledge of them from thence; and in that clear evidence we now possess them. The contrary is manifest, in the defective morality of the gentiles, before our Saviour's time; and the want of reformation in the principles and measures of it, as well as practice. Philosophy seemed to have spent its strength, and done its utmost: or if it should have gone farther, as we see it did not, and from undeniable principles given us ethics in a science like mathematics, in every part demonstrable; this yet would not have been so effectual to man in this imperfect state, nor proper for the cure. The greatest part of mankind want leisure or capacity for demonstration; nor can carry a train of proofs, which in that way they must always depend upon for conviction, and cannot be required to assent to, until they see the demonstration. Wherever they stick, the teachers are always put upon proof, and must clear the doubt by a thread of coherent deductions from the first principle, how long, or how intricate soever they be. And you may as soon hope to have all the day-labourers and tradesmen, the spinsters and dairy-maids, perfect mathematicians, as to have them perfect in ethics this way. Hearing plain commands, is the sure and only course to bring them to obedience and practice. The greatest part cannot know, and therefore they must believe. And I ask, whether one coming from heaven in the power of God, in full and clear evidence and demonstration of miracles, giving plain and direct rules of morality and obedience; be not likelier to enlighten the bulk of mankind, and set them right in their duties, and bring them to do them, than by reasoning with them from general notions and principles of human reason? And were all the duties of human life clearly demonstrated, yet I conclude, when well considered, that method of teaching men their duties would be thought proper only for a few, who had much leisure, improved understandings, and were used to abstract reasonings. But the instruction of the people were best still to be left to the precepts and principles of the gospel. The healing of the sick, the restoring sight to the blind by a word, the raising and being raised from the dead, are matters of fact, which they can without difficulty conceive, and that he who does such things, must do them by the assistance of a divine power. These things lie level to the ordinariest apprehension: he that can distinguish between sick and well, lame and sound, dead and alive, is capable of this doctrine. To one who is once persuaded that Jesus Christ was sent by God to be a King, and a Saviour of those who do believe in him; all his commands become principles; there needs no other proof for the truth of what he says, but that he said it. And then there needs no more, but to read the inspired books, to be instructed: all the duties of morality lie there clear, and plain, and easy to be understood. And here I appeal, whether this be not the surest, the safest, and most effectual way of teaching: especially if we add this farther consideration, that as it suits the lowest capacities of reasonable creatures, so it reaches and satisfies, nay, enlightens the highest. The most elevated understandings cannot but submit to the authority of this doctrine as divine; which coming from the mouths of a company of illiterate men, hath not only the attestation of miracles, but reason to confirm it: since they delivered no precepts but such, as though reason of itself had not clearly made out, yet it could not but assent to, when thus discovered, and think itself indebted for the discovery. The credit and authority our Saviour and his apostles had over the minds of men, by the miracles they did, tempted them not to mix (as we find in that of all the sects and philosophers, and other religions) any conceits, any wrong rules, any thing tending to their own by-interest, or that of a party, in their morality. No tang of prepossession, or fancy; no footsteps of pride, or vanity; no touch of ostentation, or ambition: appears to have a hand in it. It is all pure, all sincere; nothing too much, nothing wanting; but such a complete rule of life, as the wisest men must acknowledge, tends entirely to the good of mankind, and that all would be happy, if all would practise it.

3. The outward forms of worshipping the Deity, wanted a reformation. Stately buildings, costly ornaments, peculiar and uncouth habits, and a numerous huddle of pompous, fantastical, cumbersome ceremonies, every-where attended divine worship. This, as it had the peculiar name, so it was thought the principal part, if not the whole of religion. Nor could this, possibly, be amended, whilst the jewish ritual stood; and there was so much of it mixed with the worship of the true God. To this also our Saviour, with the knowledge of the infinite, invisible, supreme Spirit, brought a remedy, in a plain, spiritual, and suitable worship. Jesus says to the woman of Samaria, "The hour cometh, when ye shall neither in this mountain, nor yet at Jerusalem, worship the Father. But the true worshippers shall worship the Father, both in Spirit and in truth; for the Father seeketh such to worship him." To be worshipped in spirit and truth, with application of mind, and sincerity of heart, was what God henceforth only required. Magnificent temples, and confinement to certain places, were now no longer necessary for his worship, which by a pure heart might be performed any-where. The splendour and distinction of habits, and pomp of ceremonies, and all outside performances, might now be spared. God, who was a spirit, and made known to be so, required none of those, but the spirit only; and that in public assemblies, (where some actions must lie open to the view of the world), all that could appear

and be seen, should be done decently, and in order, and to edification. Decency, order and edification, were to regulate all their public acts of worship, and beyond what these required, the outward appearance (which was of little value in the eyes of God) was not to go. Having shut indecency and confusion out of their assemblies, they need not be solicitous about useless ceremonies. Praises and prayer, humbly offered up to the Deity, were the worship he now demanded; and in these every one was to look after his own heart, and to know that it was that alone which God had regard to, and accepted.

4. Another great advantage received by our Saviour, is the great encouragement he brought to a virtuous and pious life; great enough to surmount the difficulties and obstacles that lie in the way to it, and reward the pains and hardships of those who stuck firm to their duties, and suffered for the testimony of a good conscience. The portion of the righteous has been in all ages taken notice of, to be pretty scanty in this world. Virtue and prosperity do not often accompany one another; and therefore virtue seldom had many followers. And it is no wonder she prevailed not much in a state, where the inconveniencies that attended her were visible, and at hand; and the rewards doubtful, and at a distance. Mankind, who are and must be allowed to pursue their happiness, nay, cannot be hindered; could not but think themselves excused from a strict observation of rules, which appeared so little to consist of their chief end, happiness; whilst they kept them from the enjoyments of this life; and they had little evidence and security of another. It is true they might have argued the other way, and concluded, That because the good were most of them ill-treated here, there was another place where they should meet with better usage; but it is plain they did not: their thoughts of another life were at best obscure, and their expectations uncertain. Of manes, and ghosts, and the shades of departed men, there was some talk; but little certain, and less minded. They had the names of Styx and Acheron, of Elysian fields and seats of the blessed: but they had them generally from their poets, mixed with their fables. And so they looked more like the inventions of wit, and ornaments of poetry, than the serious persuasions of the grave and the sober. They came to them bundled up among their tales, and for tales they took them. And that which rendered them more suspected, and less useful to virtue, was, that the philosophers seldom set their rules on men's minds and practices, by consideration of another life. The chief of their arguments were from the excellency of virtue; and the highest they generally went, was the exalting of human nature, whose perfection lay in virtue. And if the priest at any time talked of the ghosts below, and a life after this; it was only to keep men to their superstitious and idolatrous rites; whereby the use of this doctrine was lost to the credulous multitude, and its belief to the quicker-sighted; who suspected it presently of priestcraft. Before our Saviour's time the doctrine of a future state, though it were not wholly hid, yet it was not clearly known in the world. It was an imperfect view of reason, or, perhaps, the decayed remains of an ancient tradition, which seemed rather to float on men's fancies, than sink deep into their hearts. It was something they knew not what, between being and not being. Something in man they imagined might escape the grave; but a perfect complete life, of an eternal duration, after this, was what entered little into their thoughts and less into their persuasions. And they were so far from being clear herein, that we see no nation of the world publicly professed it, and built upon it: no religion taught it; and it was no-where made an article of faith, and principle of religion, until Jesus Christ came; of whom it is truly said, that he, at his appearing, "brought life and immortality to light." And that not only in the clear revelation of it, and in instances shown of men raised from the dead; but he has given us an unquestionable assurance and pledge of it in his own resurrection and ascension into heaven. How has this one truth changed the nature of things

in the world, and given the advantage to piety over all that could tempt or deter men from it! The philosophers, indeed, showed the beauty of virtue; they set her off so, as drew men's eyes and approbation to her; but leaving her unendowed, very few were willing to espouse her. The generality could not refuse her their esteem and commendation; but still turned their backs on her, and forsook her, as a match not for their turn. But now there being put into the scales on her side, "an exceeding and immortal weight of glory;" interest is come about to her, and virtue now is visibly the most enriching purchase, and by much the best bargain. That she is the perfection and excellency of our nature; that she is herself a reward, and will recommend our names to future ages, is not all that can now be said of her. It is not strange that the learned heathens satisfied not many with such airy commendations. It has another relish and efficacy to persuade men, that if they live well here, they shall be happy hereafter. Open their eyes upon the endless, unspeakable joys of another life, and their hearts will find something solid and powerful to move them. The view of heaven and hell will cast a slight upon the short pleasures and pains of this present state, and give attractions and encouragements to virtue which reason and interest, and the care of ourselves, cannot but allow and prefer. Upon this foundation, and upon this only, morality stands firm, and may defy all competition. This makes it more than a name; a substantial good, worth all our aims and endeavours; and thus the gospel of Jesus Christ has delivered it to us.

5. To these I must add one advantage more by Jesus Christ, and that is the promise of assistance. If we do what we can, he will give us his Spirit to help us to do what, and how we should. It will be idle for us, who know not how our own spirits move and act us, to ask in what manner the Spirit of God shall work upon us. The wisdom that accompanies that Spirit knows better than we, how we are made, and how to work upon us. If a wise man knows how to prevail on his child, to bring him to what he desires; can we suspect that the spirit and wisdom of God should fail in it; though we perceive or comprehend not the ways of his operation? Christ has promised it, who is faithful and just; and we cannot doubt of the performance. It is not requisite on this occasion, for the enhancing of this benefit, to enlarge on the frailty of our minds, and weakness of our constitutions; how liable to mistakes, how apt to go astray, and how easily to be turned out of the paths of virtue. If any one needs go beyond himself, and the testimony of his own conscience in this point; if he feels not his own errours and passions always tempting, and often prevailing, against the strict rules of his duty; he need but look abroad into any stage of the world, to be convinced. To a man under the difficulties of his nature, beset with temptations, and hedged in with prevailing custom; it is no small encouragement to set himself seriously on the courses of virtue, and practice of true religion; that he is from a sure hand, and an Almighty arm, promised assistance to support and carry him through.

There remains yet something to be said to those, who will be ready to object, "If the belief of Jesus of Nazareth to be the Messiah, together with those concomitant articles of his resurrection, rule, and coming again to judge the world, be all the faith required, as necessary to justification, to what purpose were the epistles written; I say, if the belief of those many doctrines contained in them be not also necessary to salvation; and what is there delivered a christian may believe or disbelieve, and yet, nevertheless, be a member of Christ's church, and one of the faithful?"

To this I answer, that the epistles are written upon several occasions: and he that will read them as he ought, must observe what it is in them, which is principally aimed at; find what is the argument in hand, and how managed; if he will understand them right, and profit by them. The observing of this will best help us to the true meaning and mind of the writer; for that is the truth which is to be received and believed; and not scattered sentences in scripture-language, accommodated to our notions and prejudices. We must look into the drift of the discourse, observe the coherence and connexion of the parts, and see how it is consistent with itself and other parts of scripture; if we will conceive it right. We must not cull out, as best suits our system, here and there a period or verse; as if they were all distinct and independent aphorisms; and make these the fundamental articles of the christian faith, and necessary to salvation; unless God has made them so. There be many truths in the bible, which a good christian may be wholly ignorant of, and so not believe: which, perhaps, some lay great stress on, and call fundamental articles, because they are the distinguishing points of their communion. The epistles, most of them, carry on a thread of argument, which, in the style they are writ, cannot every-where be observed without great attention, and to consider the texts as they stand, and bear a part in that, is to view them in their due light, and the way to get the true sense of them. They were writ to those who were in the faith, and true christians already: and so could not be designed to teach them the fundamental articles and points necessary to salvation. The epistle to the Romans was writ to all "that were at Rome, beloved of God, called to be saints, whose faith was spoken of through the world," chap. i. 7, 8. To whom St. Paul's first epistle to the Corinthians was, he shows, chap. i. 2, 4, &c. "Unto the church of God which is at Corinth, to them that are sanctified in Christ Jesus, called to be saints; with all them that in every place call upon the name of Jesus Christ our Lord, both theirs and ours. I thank my God always on your behalf, for the grace of God which is given you by Jesus Christ; that in every thing ye are enriched by him, in all utterance, and in all knowledge: even as the testimony of Christ was confirmed in you. So that ye come behind in no gift; waiting for the coming of our Lord Jesus Christ." And so likewise the second was, "To the church of God at Corinth, with all the saints in Achaia," chap. i. 1. His next is to the churches of Galatia. That to the Ephesians was, "To the saints that were at Ephesus, and to the faithful in Christ Jesus." So likewise, "To the saints and faithful brethren in Christ at Colosse, who had faith in Christ Jesus, and love to the saints. To the church of the Thessalonians. To Timothy his son in the faith. To Titus his own son after the common faith. To Philemon his dearly beloved, and fellow-labourer." And the author to the Hebrews calls those he writes to "Holy brethren, partakers of the heavenly calling," chap. iii. 1. From whence it is evident, that all those whom St. Paul writ to, were brethren, saints, faithful in the church, and so christians already; and therefore, wanted not the fundamental articles of the christian religion; without a belief of which they could not be saved; nor can it be supposed, that the sending of such fundamentals was the reason of the apostle's writing to any of them. To such also St. Peter writes, as is plain from the first chapter of each of his epistles. Nor is it hard to observe the like in St. James's and St. John's epistles. And St. Jude directs his thus: "To them that are sanctified by God the Father, and preserved in Jesus Christ, and called." The epistles, therefore, being all written to those who were already believers and christians, the occasion and end of writing them could not be to instruct them in that which was necessary to make them christians. This, it is plain, they knew and believed already; or else they could not have been christians and believers. And they were writ upon particular occasions; and without those occasions, had not been writ; and so cannot be thought necessary to salvation: though they resolving doubts, and reforming mistakes, are of great advantage to our knowledge and practice. I do not deny, but the great doctrines of the christian faith are dropt here and there, and scattered up and down in most of them. But it is not in the epistles we are to learn what are the fundamental articles of faith, where they are promiscuously and without distinction mixed with other truths, in discourses that were (though for edification, indeed, yet) only occasional. We shall find and discern those great and necessary points best, in the preaching of our Saviour and the apostles, to those who were yet strangers, and ignorant of the faith; to bring them in, and convert them to it. And what that was, we have seen already, out of the history of the evangelists, and the acts; where they are plainly laid down, so that nobody can mistake them. The epistles to particular churches, besides the main argument of each of them, (which was some present concernment of that particular church, to which they severally were addressed,) do in many places explain the fundamentals of the christian religion, and that wisely; by proper accommodations to the apprehensions of those they were writ to; the better to make them imbibe the christian doctrine, and the more easily to comprehend the method, reasons, and grounds of the great work of salvation. Thus we see, in the epistle to the Romans, adoption (a custom well known amongst those of Rome) is much made use of, to explain to them the grace and favour of God, in giving them eternal life; to help them to conceive how they became the children of God, and to assure them of a share in the kingdom of heaven, as heirs to an inheritance. Whereas the setting out, and confirming the christian faith to the Hebrews, in the epistle to them, is by illusions and arguments, from the ceremonies, sacrifices, and œconomy of the jews, and references to the records of the Old Testament. And as for the general epistles, they, we may see, regard the state and exigencies, and some peculiarities of those times. These holy writers, inspired from above, writ nothing but truth; and in most places, very weighty truths to us now; for the expounding, clearing, and confirming of the christian doctrine, and establishing those in it who had embraced it. But yet every sentence of theirs must not be taken up, and looked on as a fundamental article, necessary to salvation; without an explicit belief whereof, no-body could be a member of Christ's church here, nor be admitted into his eternal kingdom hereafter. If all, or most of the truths declared in the epistles, were to be received and believed as fundamental articles, what then became of those christians who were fallen asleep (as St. Paul witnesses in his first to the Corinthians, many were) before these things in the epistles were revealed to them? Most of the epistles not being written till above twenty years after our Saviour's ascension, and some after thirty.

But farther, therefore, to those who will be ready to say, "May those truths delivered in the epistles, which are not contained in the preaching of our Saviour and his apostles, and are therefore, by this account, not necessary to salvation; be believed or disbelieved, without any danger? May a christian safely question or doubt of them?"

To this I answer, That the law of faith, being a covenant of free grace, God alone can appoint what shall be necessarily believed by every one whom he will justify. What is the faith which he will accept and account for righteousness, depends wholly on his good pleasure. For it is of grace, and not of right, that this faith is accepted. And therefore he alone can set the measures of it: and what he has so appointed and declared is alone necessary. No-body can add to these fundamental articles of faith; nor make any other necessary, but what God himself hath made, and declared to be so. And what these are which God requires of those who will enter into, and receive the benefits of the new covenant, has already been shown. An explicit belief of these is absolutely required of all those to whom the gospel of Jesus Christ is preached, and salvation through his name proposed.

The other parts of divine revelation are objects of faith, and are so to be received. They are truths, whereof no one can be rejected; none that is once known to be such, may, or ought to be disbelieved. For to acknowledge any proposition to be of divine revelation and authority; and yet to deny, or disbelieve it; is to offend against this fundamental article and ground of faith, that God is true. But yet a great many of the truths revealed in the gospel, every one does, and must confess, a man may be ignorant of; nay, disbelieve, without danger to his salvation: as is evident in those, who, allowing the authority, differ in the interpretation and meaning of several texts of scripture, not thought fundamental: in all which, it is plain, the contending parties on one side or the other, are ignorant of, nay, disbelieve the truths delivered in holy writ; unless contrarieties and contradictions can be contained in the same words; and divine revelation can mean contrary to itself.

Though all divine revelation requires the obedience of faith, yet every truth of inspired scriptures is not one of those, that by the law of faith is required to be explicitly believed to justification. What those are, we have seen by what our Saviour and his apostles proposed to, and required in those whom they converted to the faith. Those are fundamentals, which it is not enough not to disbelieve: every one is required actually to assent to them. But any other proposition contained in the scripture, which God has not thus made a necessary part of the law of faith, (without an actual assent to which, he will not allow any one to be a believer,) a man may be ignorant of, without hazarding his salvation by a defect in his faith. He believes all that God has made necessary for him to believe, and assent to; and as for the rest of divine truths, there is nothing more required of him, but that he receive all the parts of divine revelation, with a docility and disposition prepared to embrace and assent to all truths coming from God; and submit his mind to whatsoever shall appear to him to bear that character. Where he, upon fair endeavours, understands it not, how can he avoid being ignorant? And where he cannot put several texts, and make them consist together, what remedy? He must either interpret one by the other, or suspend his opinion. He that thinks that more is, or can be required of poor frail man in matters of faith, will do well to consider what absurdities he will run into. God, out of the infiniteness of his mercy, has dealt with man, as a compassionate and tender Father. He gave him reason, and with it a law: that could not be otherwise than what reason should dictate: unless we should think, that a reasonable creature should have an unreasonable law. But, considering the frailty of man, apt to run into corruption and misery, he promised a Deliverer, whom in his good time he sent; and then declared to all mankind, that whoever would believe him to be the Saviour promised, and take him now raised from the dead, and constituted the Lord and Judge of all men, to be their King and Ruler, should be saved. This is a plain intelligible proposition: and the all-merciful God seems herein to have consulted the poor of this world, and the bulk of mankind. These are articles that the labouring and illiterate man may comprehend. This is a religion suited to vulgar capacities; and the state of mankind in this world, destined to labour and travel. The writers and wranglers in religion fill it with niceties, and dress it up with notions, which they make necessary and fundamental parts of it; as if there were no way into the church, but through the academy or lyceum. The greatest part of mankind have not leisure for learning and logic, and superfine distinctions of the schools. Where the hand is used to the plough and the spade, the head is seldom elevated to sublime notions, or exercised in mysterious reasoning. It is well if men of that rank (to say nothing of the other sex) can comprehend plain propositions, and a short reasoning about things familiar to their minds, and nearly allied to their daily experience. Go beyond this, and you amaze the greatest part of mankind; and may as well talk Arabic to a poor day-labourer, as the notions and language that the books and disputes of religion are filled with; and as soon you will be understood. The dissenting congregation are supposed by their teachers to be more accurately instructed in matters of faith, and better to understand the christian religion, than the vulgar conformists, who are charged with great ignorance; how truly, I will not here determine. But I ask them to tell me seriously, "Whether half their people have leisure to study? Nay, Whether one in ten, of those who come to their meetings in the country, if they had time to study them, do or can understand the controversies at this time so warmly managed amongst them, about 'justification,' the subject of this present treatise?" I have talked with some of their teachers, who confess themselves not to understand the difference in debate between them. And yet the points they stand on, are reckoned of so great weight; so material, so fundamental in religion, that they divide communion, and separate upon them. Had God intended that none but the learned scribe, the disputer, or wise of this world, should be christians, or be saved, thus religion should have been prepared for them, filled with speculations and niceties, obscure terms, and abstract notions. But men of that expectation, men furnished with such acquisitions, the apostle tells us, 1 Cor. i. are rather shut out from the simplicity of the gospel; to make way for those poor, ignorant, illiterate, who heard and believed promises of a Deliverer, and believed Jesus to be him; who could conceive a man dead and made alive again; and believe that he should, at the end of the world, come again and pass sentence on all men, according to their deeds. That the poor had the gospel preached to them; Christ makes a mark, as well as business of his mission, Matt. xi. 5. And if the poor had the gospel preached to them, it was, without doubt, such a gospel as the poor could understand; plain and intelligible: and so it was, as we have seen, in the preachings of Christ and his apostles.

CPSIA information can be obtained at www.ICGtesting.com
Printed in the USA
LVOW10s1813040916

503183LV00030B/432/P